NEC'S 2014.

COSMIC
RELATIONSHIPS

To Ray,
Surprise !

Exploring the Soul's Journey from Off-Earth, Earth Lives, and Reincarnation

Based on the Athor Readings, Religious Research Readings, and Personal Experiences

Love,
Rev. Kar Lee Samson

Rev Karen L Samson
4149 NW 12th Ter
Ft Lauderdale, FL 33309

COSMIC RELATIONSHIPS

EVELYN FUQUA PH.D.

O.M.R.A. – Bandon, Oregon
2012

Dedicated to all those who continually search for the truth
regarding human relationships.

Acknowledgements

My deep appreciation to Aki, Athor and the Council of Twelve on the etheric plane of the star system of Sirius; my friends at Religious Research, and all of my husbands who contributed greatly to my own evolution in this lifetime. I am most grateful to Dr. Leo Sprinkle for having enough faith in me to again review one of my books. Dr. Sprinkle was very influential in my earlier quest to understand Extraterrestrials; Deep appreciation to my dear friend Linda Pendleton for her kind review of the book and also giving me valuable guidance in the publishing process. I am deeply indebted to my friend Michael Phelan for taking the time to review this book. In addition, Michael was of immeasurable assistance in publishing my book. My thanks to Maria Phelan, who did proof reading, and prepared astrology charts for Paul and myself. Both Michael and Maria have been supportive friends ever since we 'discovered' each other shortly after my move to Bandon.

My publisher, OMRA, has encouraged me to use the extensive research conducted by Oakdell Multidimensional Research Association composed of many Light workers who met in my office complex monthly for ten years.

Most of all my love and gratitude to my mate Paul Mounts who has encouraged me to write this book, and given me technical advice as well as authoring a portion of his own story. He has given me loving emotional support throughout this endeavor.

Table of Contents

Preface

A week before Christmas in 1988 a woman came to me for assistance in helping her overcome a life threatening condition of environmental illness. I had never had any experience with this kind of problem before and seriously doubted if I could help her. As she told me later, she had seen my photograph in a metaphysical magazine and was told (psychically) that I was the person who could help her so she was extremely insistent that I become her therapist. I became even more apprehensive about working with her when I learned during our first session that she had been institutionalized with the diagnosis of paranoid schizophrenia when she was in college. She did not impress me as being psychotic, so after insisting that she sign a release of liability form, I decided to schedule at least one additional therapy session to see if indeed there was any way that I could help her.

That one session extended into months of intensive therapy; then intermittent sessions for three full years. Shortly into the therapy sessions, we discovered that when Rose, my client, was three years, two months old there appeared to be a soul exchange with one aspect of a member of the Council of Twelve on the etheric plane of the star system Sirius.

I had been a past life regression therapist for a number of years but this was certainly a new issue for me in my therapy work. First I ruled out possession; the Athor being was welcomed into the body of the child Rose; it was not taken over as in cases of possession. Next I considered the possibility of Rose/Athor being a multiple personality (disassociated personality.) Neither of these seemed to be the case. It also became clear to me that the therapy was probably not going to cure the environmental illness. However, I became

i

intrigued with trying to discover why this highly enlightened being would make an agreement to come into an extremely damaged body. Rose came from a very dysfunctional family background, which added to the puzzle. We agreed to continue the therapy as a research project for no fee. The unraveling of all the many pieces of information which came through slowly in no particular order resulted in our co-authoring the book, *From Sirius to Earth: a Therapist Discovers a Soul Exchange,* which was published in 1997. It is a combination of the therapy process along with an autobiography by Athor.

During the process of the therapy sessions, I discovered that Athor had remarkable psychic abilities. Although my career for the past eighteen years as a Marriage, Family Therapist specializing in past life regression therapy had been devoted to working with highly evolved, exceptionally spiritual people, I am ever the skeptic so I decided to conduct further research on readings that she did for my clients. I always took a case history of my clients and then, of course, found out a great deal about them as therapy progressed. When my client and I had reached a point in the process of hypnotherapy where I felt we had gone about as far as we could go in effectively overcoming their problems, I often suggested they consider an Athor reading. I never told Athor anything about the client ahead of time since I didn't want her to have any preconceived ideas before the reading. Usually the clients would come with a list of questions which were of particular importance to them. From the beginning she had never wanted any prior information; she told me that she didn't want to clutter her mind with unnecessary verbiage. As a researcher I always wanted to see if the information in the reading matched my impression of the client from a therapist's point of view.

I have always been amazed at the accuracy of how the readings 'fit' the clients, but the information went far beyond anything I had discovered through the therapy process. Athor addressed the core issues of the problems from a soul point of view. This is the kind of information and understanding that probably would never have surfaced even after years of therapy. Many of the readings seemed like science fiction, but having great faith in the integrity of the readings, I was not shocked at much of anything anymore as I have continued learning more about the complicated path of the soul.

I have personally known only one other person whom I felt was able to give readings that were comparable to the Athor readings. Dr. Franklin Loehr of Religious Research in Grand Island, Florida was able to go into a trance and access Dr. John Christopher Daniels, a spirit guide who specialized in reading the Akashic records. Dr. Loehr, born in 1912, was a pioneer in bringing religion into the Age of Science. Through the years after joining Religious Research, I became personally acquainted with Dr. Loehr and other staff members of his organization. The many excellent books published by Religious Research, along with my conviction of the strong personal integrity and brilliant mind of Dr. Loehr, were a strong influence in my acceptance of reincarnation. Although Franklin has made his transition from the Earth plane, I feel that his readings, just as the Edgar Cayce readings, have contributed greatly in assisting many millions of people to believe in the validity of past lives and the overall cosmic scheme of the universe. I view the Cayce work as the beginning of valid channel information, the Loehr work as a continuance and elaboration of similar research and the Athor readings as a third step in understanding the soul. The Athor readings are unique in that they often refer to past existences on other planets, other dimensions, etc. In this book, through Athor, I also delve into life after death and the planning of a rebirth, all the way into another reincarnation.

I particularly appreciated the Loehr and Cayce readings because of their strong association with Christ. When I first began conducting past life regressions in my private practice, I wanted my clients to know that I have a strong faith in the Christ Consciousness and believe Jesus Christ to be one of the great Ascended Masters. Many of my clients came from Catholic backgrounds, as well as various other religious backgrounds. Most of them were struggling with the need for a spiritual belief system that incorporated their belief in past lives as well as their faith in the master Jesus Christ. It was apparent during the therapy process with Rose/Athor that she too had a strong association with God and the Christ Consciousness. I, therefore, felt comfortable in having Athor do readings for my clients since I sensed that she was a deeply spiritual person.

From the beginning we approached the readings from a spiritual viewpoint. We used the same basic hypnotic induction that I had used for many years, but the invocation just prior to the reading was changed a number of times since she would get a message at various points that some of the wording needed to be different. Back in 1992 the induction simply consisted of the following: "And now we ask for a lineup with the Ray of Life between 3rd and 4th density, bringing with it the octave of wisdom at the 11th sub octave level between 5th and 6th densities. May we begin?" We later progressed to a much more complicated induction: "In the Light of the fusion and the blending of the three, we ask for the highest wisdom, clarity, love and assistance from all those

Beings of Light of the 10th subatomic level of alchemical transmutation. We ask above all for the Love aspect to pave the way for the greatest clarity and healing at this time. We ask for the octave of wisdom of the 12th sub octave level between 5th and 6th densities. Let the flow of the All begin." We always closed with the following statement, "Returning to the center of the life force residing between 3rd and 4th density, returning through the center of the heart." On the few occasions when Athor spontaneously came out of the trance state without these instructions, she became dizzy and disoriented. I learned to never touch her when she was in a trance state because any touch had the effect of an electrical shock.

Unfortunately when Rose/Athor moved farther up into the mountains, away from my office, we gradually discontinued the readings. Her physical condition had also continued to deteriorate, but the main problem was her vision. She had developed severe cataracts in both eyes and was slowly going blind. She felt that cataract surgery was out of the question due to her extreme allergic reactions to any anesthesia or medication. She was, therefore, no longer able to drive to my office for the readings. However, many other factors were involved which will be explored in the Introduction.

Having been a Marriage, Family Therapist for 36 years it is my hope that this book will help you better understand your own relationships. Although I will be writing about my relationships in the context of my past lives with the important men in my life, perhaps you, the reader, will see yourself with similar situations. Through knowing about my past life relationships you can surmise that you became involved with certain people because of your soul connections in past lives. While each person's story is different, people usually come together because they have some karmic issues to hopefully be resolved in this lifetime, or our partner/friend/mate is someone to assist us along our life's path.

Most of the books written about soul relationships seem to be written toward the goal of finding the perfect "soul mate." However, we have many possible soul mates. These are people we have known in past lives with each soul playing a different role. One may be the father of the other in one lifetime; in other lifetimes they often switch roles and one may be a sister, brother, another relative or even a good friend. Sometimes they are husband and wife, or lovers in a past life. When this is the case these can be intense relationships when they meet again, particularly if one or the other died prematurely and they did not have the experience of growing old together.

The sanskaras in our auric field draw us to another person somewhat like a magnet. These are the seeds of karma that we carry from one lifetime to another, although they may be dormant in some lifetimes, because we may need a lifetime of rest after going through a series of very difficult lifetimes with much soul growth. Difficult lifetimes can result in much soul growth if the personalities of those lifetimes handle the challenges in a positive manner.

When souls are truly compatible there can be the rare relationships where the two have the good fortune to meet again as a "gift" from the universe. I feel in my case that this finally happened when I met Paul at the age of 78. Although my first three husbands were all soul mates in a sense, having shared past lives together there was a difference in my past life patterns between these men and Paul. We are an example of souls who for various reasons in past lives did not complete life cycles together; therefore, there is a strong pull to try again to reach a stage of completion.

I have found that the most emotionally intense relationships are those in which the two have known each other Off-Earth. They probably have had past lives together on the Earth as well, but the intensity which can be totally irrational stems from Off-Earth existences. Besides Paul, I have had two other relationships such as this, and I have had some clients who had similar irrational feelings about someone who was totally inappropriate as far as an in-depth relationship was concerned. If the present life circumstances are not right for a relationship, the situation can be very difficult to handle. There may be a vast age difference, they live too far apart, one is married; the various circumstances can go on and on as to why these are not appropriate relationships for this particular lifetime.

I was extremely fortunate to meet Paul, but if we had met earlier in this lifetime we both agree that we may not have been particularly attracted to each other, or if we were, the relationship would probably not have gone anywhere because the timing was not right.

While the major focus of this book is on past life relationships on Earth, I am including some very extensive Athor readings which we called "Source Readings," because they trace the soul from the time it splits off from the Source, or All That Is (Godhead, whatever terminology one would like to use,) and traces its evolution until it reaches Earth. These read like science fiction, but as totally strange as they may sound, I am convinced of the accuracy of these readings.

I conducted this kind of reading for many of my clients, and while there are many similarities, each one was quite different. It seems important at this time in the history of the Earth that we have some proof that there is no conflict between evolution and creationism. As I cautioned in my first book, *From Sirius to Earth*, believe only what seems to ring true for you at a soul level. I feel that these readings were given by the Council of Sirius to humankind so we could understand that both of these concepts are valid. While this is my soul history, I don't sense a personal attachment to it, and feel it should be shared with others. Please keep in mind that these soul histories are far from complete histories; that would take many volumes to cover. The readings presented in this book are meant to give a better understanding of particular personalities in this lifetime. The personalities may be quite different in a future lifetime; although the soul will have evolved if it has handled its lessons well.

As in my former book, *From Sirius to Earth*, the real Earth name of Aki/Athor is not used to protect her privacy. To tell her story from the beginning I used the name Rose for the person who first came to me for therapy. When I discovered that what I thought then was a "soul exchange," I usually called her Athor, the name of the member of the Council of Sirius who was the soul exchange. Now, although the new personality is called Aki, I will simply still use the name Athor when giving material from the readings. No doubt some of the material is a mixture of information from Athor, plus Aki, who is also extremely psychic. I hope I do not confuse you, but the name thing had become ludicrous at times since I wasn't exactly sure to whom I was talking!

Introduction

I was very busy with my continued private practice after my late husband Wally died of leukemia. After Athor's move farther up into the mountains I rarely saw her. I was not doing much distance driving, so I was only able to visit her at her new home once, and it was a difficult drive over quite hilly, winding, gravel roads.

Athor and I would talk about once a month on the telephone, and I sensed that life was becoming increasingly difficult for her. Through my monthly metaphysical meetings Athor met Lydia (not her real name), who became a very dear friend to Athor and her daughter. Lydia also is very psychic; she and Athor would have numerous in-depth conversations in which both would go into a trance state. I was quite pleased with the relationship because it was obvious that Lydia had a deep soul connection with the Athor being. I frankly felt I had done my share for human kind in writing about the Athor Soul Exchange (a type of Walk-In experiment) in *From Sirius to Earth*. Besides, I am not nearly as psychic as Lydia; therefore, Athor and Lydia were a good match on a mental level to continue the Athor saga.

Finally in 2005 Lydia told me that Athor had "walked out". Athor had received a message that she was going to die, which she had already told me. The Earth personality of Athor/Rose had thought she was going to die many times over the years I had known her, due to her many physical problems. I, therefore, didn't take this information too seriously. Lydia and Athor had many sessions trying to figure out what indeed had happened. The "Walk-Out" episode was on October 24, 2004.

When Lydia finally understood what had happened she was devastated because her soul connection was with the

Athor being, not the being who was left behind in the physical body. It took a great deal of understanding and compassion for her to continue her friendship with Rose who at that point was a new personality. Also, about that time Rose's husband realized that Athor had walked out and the marital problems escalated. He had married the personality Athor. Both he and Lydia felt deserted. In my research with many Walk-Ins I found that these experiments often resulted in many conflicts, particularly within the family. There are various types of Walk-In experiences with many different explanations from a cosmic viewpoint, a subject much too complicated to discuss in this book. A soul exchange such as the Athor case is rather rare.

This was a time of great confusion for Rose (or whoever she was). It took many months with her friend Lydia's assistance for me to finally conclude that indeed Athor was no longer there, and to determine why Athor left. It was not an overnight "aha" moment of revelation, but many sessions between the two that finally brought Rose the peace that is akin to the feeling she experienced when she was in therapy with me and finally realized that she was Athor, not Rose. The soul exchange had taken place when the child Rose was three years, two months old on July 9, 1952; the walk out occurred when she was 55 years old.

When Lydia gave me the news of Athor leaving I didn't really want to believe this. Much earlier two other fascinating women had come to me for hypnotherapy. These were unpaid research studies that were each only one long session. They claimed to have had Walk-In experiences twice and each time the Walk-In walked out and a new personality entered the body. Since these were one session cases I thought they were interesting, but I had great difficulty believing this walk-out event actually happened. I certainly didn't want to accept the fact that Athor had walked out. I had given numerous talks and workshops at state and international conferences about my work with Athor, plus writing professional articles about this case. In addition, the book I wrote listed Athor as my co-author. To say the least I was not happy about this at all! I felt deserted and somewhat betrayed.

In the meantime I had tripped on some steps in 2005. Two broken ankles prevented me from walking for a month; I decided that this was a signal from the universe that it was time for me to retire from private practice.

For some time my current husband, Ed, had wanted to move to Oregon, away from the heat and congestion in the Central Valley of California. It had been difficult for me to take enough time away from my clients in order to explore the state of Oregon and make a decision as to the best place for us to move. The 'broken ankle' episode was the major factor in my decision to finally retire since I was not able to see my clients for about three months, and that is no way to conduct therapy. As soon as I was able to walk fairly well, Ed and I took a long trip north exploring many different possibilities of places to live in Oregon. We both fell in love with Bandon, a beautiful little town on the southern coast of Oregon. That was 2005; the process of actually making the final move was not until July 2008.

Even prior to my retirement I was no longer having Athor do readings for my clients because I was not sure Athor was still in a human body. However, as time went on I had personal questions about our move. I had felt I was out of the loop in this walk-out process since my contact with Athor had been minimal after I met Ed. I was feeling the desire to try and understand what happened from a practical viewpoint, so began requesting readings for myself to get more information about this latest experiment. Athor's friend, Lydia, had a demanding fulltime job. She had many health problems herself; therefore, I didn't feel I could bother her with many of the Athor issues.

I subsequently requested a number of telephone sessions with the former Athor, whom I discovered is now Aki. Over a period of time I had become totally convinced that Athor indeed had left the body of my former client Rose. The Aki personality is quite different from the Athor personality. Athor was very demanding and felt she was always right about everything. She was so determined to understand her entire 'experiment' that her previous sessions with me, and our extended telephone conversations were all about Athor. She radiated a strong masculine energy.

At one point, to give the readers of our book an idea of how Athor would appear if we could see him/her, I had asked for a description. Although the beings on the Council of Sirius are androgynous, the description depicted a decidedly tall male figure. Rose/Athor had also received a message stating what ATHOR stood for: Alien Through Holographic Orbital Resonance. I don't understand this, and being Athor's therapist was certainly not an easy undertaking! I loved Athor, but frequently found it difficult to like her. However, the wisdom and knowledge coming through her readings were remarkable. The vibration of the Aki personality is much gentler; she frequently wants to know about what is happening in my life, which is quite a change. Having been involved with Athor for over fifteen years, I am continuing to try and understand more about the Aki personality.

I requested a reading on January 7, 2006. After asking a few personal questions about me, we then began an exploration of Aki.

Evelyn: What has happened to Athor?
Aki: The individualized essence which came through
this vehicle in this cycle called Athor, merged into the
All That Is (Athor's name for the Godhead) on October
24, 2004.
Evelyn: Is Athor still on the Council of Sirius, or has just
this one aspect (Athor) of the Council evolved and
gone back into the All That Is?
Aki: Yes and no. It is difficult to explain, but the whole
Council, all the members have evolved. It is in a sense
not the same Council. They are still the same beings,
yet not the same beings. Everyone has evolved, so it is
a very different scenario than what you see on this
planet. When we say that the Council has evolved and
the beings are not necessarily the same ones, that
does not mean that they are different ones as you
would understand here on Earth. It is an energetic
evolution which changes not only beings but systems.
This was a slated evolutionary growth. It is an ongoing
evolution of the Council and the Council members.
Athor was the representative on this plane for the
duration of this short life cycle. She was a
spokesperson for the Council, although not in a public
sense (meaning through her readings and the book,
From Sirius to Earth). The Council has gone on to other
levels, not simply Athor.
Evelyn: So Athor had taken care of all the karma that
she/he had incurred? (Athor attempted to be a soul
exchange during the time of Jesus the Christ in order to
be of assistance to "her brother", but she did not have

the Council's permission to do this, and the Athor entity's vibrations were too high. This resulted in the death of the fetus she tried to enter, plus the death of the mother; this left a huge karmic debt for Athor. Much earlier we had received the information that the selection of the Rose body with her environmental illness and other health issues, plus the dysfunctional family, were all part of the plan for Athor to experience a broad range of negative emotions. One purpose of this soul exchange was to have the Council of Sirius understand the tremendous negativity here on Earth, and the 48 years that Athor was in the Rose body was ample time to understand this. She/he seemed to attract negativity - not what you would expect from a Being of Light, but it was all part of the cosmic plan...)

Aki: Yes.

Evelyn: When did Aki enter the Rose body?

Aki: It was seen that the personality needed an identity. The human part of this being, the cellular components of this expression needed an identity. It was when that question of identity was posed to the All That Is that the name came forth. It is not the same at all as Athor coming as an individualized identity to reside through this vehicle and function through this vehicle. That was the Athor situation. This is different. This is an evolving process that is different. What is present in this body is the conglomeration of the cellular make up and cellular memories of the Rose being, the emotional remnants and emotional patterns of the mental format and template which was expanded with Athor and by the Athor energies.

Evelyn: Then this is not a soul exchange or any kind of

Walk-In experiment.
Aki: That is correct.

There was never a complete exchange with the Rose entity when she was a child. This was an experiment sanctioned by the Council, and the vibrations needed to be gradually introduced into the physical body of the child Rose. There was a much larger infusion of energy which occurred during an out of body experience when Rose was in college. While these high vibrations created many physical problems for Rose, apparently the Council wanted to make sure the body did not actually die from this experiment. The final infusion apparently never took place, but there were enough vibrations anchored to be considered a soul exchange, or at least that is what we thought. In retrospect considering the "walk-out" occurrence, I think I would now consider this as one of the many varieties of "walk-in" experiments.

Evelyn: When Athor left and there was the feeling that no essence was embodied, how did that feel?
Aki: Very confusing. There was a great sense of an emptiness and loss because it is seen that some identifiable presence, if only through the mind and emotions, is necessary on this plane. Before that, with the absence of the Athor essence, there was simply the vastness of space and a feeling of drifting and floating, without any connection to Earth except the knowledge and the memory that there was still a body alive and functional on some levels. But there was really no connection to any human type of understanding. This brain and the cells needed that connection. Since the physical vehicle has not completed its allotted time, so

to speak, the connection to the Aki energy was formed. The Aki energy certainly is very different, very pleasant, very nice, and very different from the Athor energy.

Evelyn: After *From Sirius to Earth* was published, I received many letters and e-mails from people all over the world asking what went wrong with the Earth since the original blueprint (matrix) for the Earth (which was designed by the Council of Sirius) was planned as a pristine, spiritual planet.

Aki: It is seen that there is no definitive bottom line answer to one specific incident in answer to that question. Rather, it was a combination of many different factors. There were factions that created genetic mutations, genetic splicings. There were things tampered with in the original blueprint and that is basically what went wrong. The original blueprint did not take into account all these various splicings and mutations, and what not that could occur both ethereally as well as physically as a consequence of the blueprint being so altered. (Earlier information discussed a defective genetic component that was built into the human race as the result of the splicings and mutations.) And so it is these factors with which the Council was concerned and involved. It is seen that it has now come to an understanding of the energetic permutations which occurred in this process, and consequently, as a result of this understanding of these permutations, this Council and other Councils involved are also in a position to safeguard this type of occurrence in any future creations. That study has been completed as the result of the Earth incarnation of the Athor being.

I want to clarify a statement on page I of *From Sirius to Earth*. "There exists upon or within Sirius something akin to the Garden of Eden. There is a Council of Elders, a group of beings who gather to determine who should be created and when." Once when I was on a radio program and listeners were calling in with questions, a woman wanted to know if it really was true that the Sirian Council creates souls, which this implies. I finally was able to ask Athor about this.

> Athor: Our council, as part of the greater councils of 112 beings from this galaxy, who are only some of the Creator Gods, has been and is involved in creating different species in different systems. The greater Councils at large, not the Sirian Council, is responsible for the creation of humanity. Therefore, the word "Who" was used to indicate the entire 112 beings of the greater councils who comprised only some of the Creator Gods in this galactic system.

To clarify this further: Repeatedly when I have been having conversations with Athor both in and out of a trance state and I ask her about the creation of souls, she emphasizes that we all come from the same source. I love the following quote from Athor:

> Athor: It is wise for all to remember that we are all brothers and sisters. From the so-called lowliest forms of life upon this plane that many of you step upon when you are walking across the earth, the weeds, the grasses, the plants or the rocks you stumble upon on

your path – all of these, from that to the animals, to the human kingdom, to the angelic, the devic, and other forms of Light Beings, even beyond, and beyond, and beyond. All are the same, for we have all come from the same source. Yet each of us has taken but a slightly different path in our attempt to explore, to learn and to engage in the divine play which the All That Is has allowed us to participate in, which the All has created in its totality. If we but remember that we are indeed all the same, that your neighbor who pisses you off, as it were, one day and then may need your help another, that neighbor with his or her particular emotions, and you with your particular emotions, are all the same. Your emotions are not you. It is often most difficult for you on this plane to recognize that reality, as indeed you have for so long resonated to the frequency of emotion. One, who is termed a young soul according to earth lives, can be ageless from the original source with many other experiences elsewhere not on this Earth. (This last statement is not an exact Athor quote, but paraphrased since it came from the contents of a reading for a particular client who felt she was a young soul.)

People have said to me, "You must be an old soul". Yes, I suppose I am, in terms of Earth and Off-Earth lives. However, I have always dodged that question because Athor was very opposed to inflating the ego of anyone who wanted to know if they are an old soul. That can too easily be an ego trip for those who are old souls. However, Religious Research actually divided souls into five stages from the beginning (just touching down on Earth and often dying quite young) up to old soul. Their soul research was basically a research project, all of the data being transcribed, each reading being given a number for confidentiality and then the information was used for numerous books based on the readings. Identifying the age of the soul in terms of Earth lives seemed to be important to the research.

Back in 1970, when I first requested a reading from Dr. John at Religious Research, he identified me as a soul well along. I feel that I have evolved quite a bit since then through my work with Athor; however, I know there are many more people on Earth much more evolved than I am. We are all a work in progress. The evolutionary process goes on and on ...and on! If you are an older soul, you have volunteered to be here on Earth to help younger souls with their evolvement, which is often not an easy task as you will see in the case of my second husband, Wally. We all have free choice, therefore, even though there are certain lessons each of us should hopefully learn in each incarnation, we may choose not to follow the paths that will accomplish this.

Chapter 1

Decision to Write This Book

Evelyn in her office, 1990

All of the information about the Rose/Athor/Aki story is very esoteric and difficult for many people to understand. However, a brief discussion of her story was necessary to establish the background for this book. I have delayed writing another book for many reasons but mainly I had not been able to decide how to condense and make sense out of all the hundreds of readings I conducted with Athor for my clients. I was still mulling this over when I heard from a good friend, Linda Pendleton, about Dr. Peebles.

Linda and her late husband, Don Pendleton had written a book about Dr. Peebles, a spirit guide, entitled *To Dance with Angels*. I decided to have a reading from him through one of Linda's friends, Athena Demetrios, a trance channel. I asked him about my writing another book. His advice was to make it more personal than the first book. I am a very private person so this didn't particularly resonate with me at the time. I wrote the first few chapters of a proposed book entitled *"Our ET Heritage"* but it never seemed to go very far so that was put on the shelf for a number of years. In the meantime, I discovered that Athor had left the Earth plane and I began to question the whole Athor saga so at that time I was reluctant to write a book strictly based on the Athor readings. I also remembered that Athor had told me that each reading was done at the request of different individuals so I should use caution in inferring that what is true for one soul is true for all souls. I still feel that there are many universal truths in the readings since certain questions would trigger a long explanation which certainly to me seemed as if it were valuable information for the masses.

There may be another book using many of the Athor readings; however, at this point I am going to take the advice that is given to many writers and as Dr. Peebles implied, "Write about what you know best". What I know best are the soul journeys of myself, my three husbands and my present Soul Mate. At the age of 79 I have decided that perhaps my understandings about my relationships will help other people better understand their relationship with people in their lives.

While everyone's story is different, we are all expressions of the Creator. Through deep meditation everyone can sense their relationship with the people close to them. While helpful, it is not necessary to have a reading from a psychic. The Earth is rapidly evolving and it is time to know that from creation, souls have a long evolutionary path and it will continue many eons after they have left the body here on Earth. The plan for creation is to continue evolving just as the Council of Sirius evolved.

  While it would probably be helpful for one to have read my previous book, *From Sirius to Earth*, this should not be necessary to understand the concepts in this book. My intention is to write a much more Earth oriented book to which many of you can relate in regard to your own soul relationships.

CHAPTER 2

Carroll, My Industrial Engineer Husband

Carroll

Two years after I graduated from college I met my first husband, Carroll, on a blind date. I was teaching at that time in Atlanta, Georgia in a school which was in the growing Buckhead area of the city. I had forty students in my third grade classroom. My B.A. degree from nearby Agnes Scott

College was in psychology. Although Agnes Scott has continued to be a highly academic college, my mental programming at the time in 1953 was: "School teaching is the most suitable occupation for a girl until she gets married and has a family."

Many of my classmates were already married, but I had dated very little in college and had little opportunity to meet men in my role as a teacher. Carroll had been in the Army for three years and was attending Georgia Tech on the GI bill. He was obviously very intelligent, making straight A's when we first met. I was a virgin at 23, with almost no sexual experience. There was a strong physical attraction from the beginning and Carroll took full advantage of this.

After my family decided we were in a serious relationship, they invited him to our home in a small town about 100 miles south of Atlanta. This did not go well. They had someone investigate his family who lived further south in Georgia and discovered that they were definitely not in the upper social strata as my family in Fort Valley had been for many years. They informed me that I would be disinherited if I married Carroll. They thought that he was mainly interested in me because of the money that I would supposedly one day inherit. His father worked for the local undertaker in the town where he was born, and his mother made some extra money being a seamstress. It was a very dysfunctional family with Carroll's mother laying a tremendous amount of responsibility on Carroll, the oldest of three children.

Carroll and I had spent a weekend with his parents and even met his grandmother. They all seemed to be very nice people as far as I could tell. Even though I was born in 1932 while this country was still in a deep depression and my parents always watched money very closely, I had never

6

experienced any real material need. I was making $2,500 a year teaching, paying all my expenses (rent $75 split with my roommate) and even saving money, so to me finances were simply not a big consideration in getting married. However, Carroll was still in college and not able to support us, so this was totally against the values of my parents. My father's parents were some of the early founders of my small town in Georgia and my mother was devoted to the DAR (Daughters of the American Revolution). We were at the top of the social scale such as it is in a small Southern town. This was definitely not the case with Carroll's family although interestingly, all three children in his family graduated from college and were successful in their chosen careers (two engineers, one teacher).

I had been the "good" girl in high school. The boy I went steady with never even kissed me, and that was fine with me. The mother of the girl that all the boys liked was very happy about our relationship because she felt I was a positive influence on her rather wild daughter. One of the main reasons for my sterling reputation was because during my junior year I had fallen very much in love with another boy who had dropped out of school to join the Air Force. My parents did not think he was suitable for me and they made that quite clear. In addition he was having many conflicts with his stepfather, thus his decision to leave the area. I lived for his letters during my senior year and even after going off to college, but I finally heard that he had married and was working at the Pentagon. He was extremely intelligent and ended up being the west coast sales manager for IBM. I never forgot about George and am sure we will meet again in a future life.

George and I had never been sexually involved, so once I finally discovered sex with Carroll I was ready to rebel against my sheltered background. I had decided that my parents were never going to approve of anyone who really attracted me. They tried to set me up with various boys from "good" families in Fort Valley but those dates always fell flat. Besides, my family felt that since I was obviously sexually involved with Carroll that I was ruined for any other man, so they finally encouraged me to marry him even though they refused to come to our wedding in Atlanta.

After graduating from Georgia Tech in 1955, Carroll accepted a job with the National Security Agency in Washington DC, and we moved to nearby Silver Spring MD. Before accepting the job he was flown to Washington DC for several weeks of "briefing". At that time I knew absolutely nothing about the National Security Agency (NSA) or extraterrestrials, but in retrospect I believe he was told in that briefing about the government having alien space craft and part of his job was determining the most efficient method of transporting the bodies, and perhaps pieces of the wreckages. Carroll had by then switched his major from electrical engineering to industrial engineering, which deals with job efficiency.

I recently found an article in the Mutual UFO Journal which probably explains some of the pressures of the briefing that Carroll went through in Washington at NSA. In his book *Skunk Works*, author Leo Janos cited a conversation between Kelly Johnson, the founder of Skunk Works (developer of secret military aircraft) and Rich Johnson, director of Skunk Works from 1975-1991. "Rich, this project (the U-2 spy plane) is so secret that you may have a six-month to one-year hole in your resume that can never be filled in. Whatever you learn, see, and hear for as long as you work inside this building stays forever inside this building. Is that clear? You'll tell no one about what we do or what you do not; this includes your wife, your mother, your brother, your girlfriend, your priest, or your CPA. You got that straight? OK, first read over this briefing disclosure form, which says what I've just said, only in 'governmentese.' Just remember, having a big mouth will cost you 20 years in Leavenworth, minimum." If, in fact, Carroll had a similar conversation during his briefing at NSA; I can only imagine how difficult that must have been to keep government secrets, particularly if it actually involved extraterrestrials and not spy planes. I remember that he seemed quite disturbed after his trip to Washington but the only explanation he would give me was that they wanted to make sure that he was not a homosexual. That didn't make much sense to me, but I accepted it at the time.

Although Carol seemingly did not like his job with NSA, he continued in various government type positions until he eventually retired due to heart problems. He seemed to become quite paranoid at times after we moved to California, suspecting that people were following him. By then he was working for McClellan Air Force Materials Base in Sacramento. While still there he was suddenly sent to Hawaii for three months, with no explanation to me as to the purpose of this trip. I had no idea what was going on with him and he offered no rational explanations. Before he left for Hawaii we had our house up for sale and had a buyer. I was left with the task of cleaning the house for the new owner, moving, and getting settled in an apartment.

Shortly after the move, John F. Kennedy was assassinated. I remember sitting in front of the television set for hours watching the funeral, etc. I was exhausted and very depressed. However, I had a new job as a counselor at a high school that had just opened, and the head counselor was an angel who helped me immensely. I was the first person in my district that had ever been hired as a high school counselor without any teaching experience at that level, and I needed a lot of help, never having experienced the scheduling challenges of a high school counselor. I was an excellent counselor as far as student relationships were concerned, but soon learned that one of my main jobs was scheduling, enrolling new students, paperwork galore, etc., things I knew nothing about.

Dick, my head counselor was a blonde, extremely good looking, charismatic man who later became director of personnel for my very large school district. I had a huge crush on Dick, and I think it was mutual but we were both married, so anything more than a professional relationship was out of the question.

While Carroll was in Hawaii and I had finally recovered from my trying moving experience, I begin to find that I was enjoying life more. This was the first time I had ever lived alone, having gone from a roommate after college then getting married. I think the idea of living alone was rather daunting and probably one reason I had remained married. When Carroll returned from Hawaii, we moved into a two bedroom apartment upstairs in the same complex.

The following year I decided that I really wanted to go to Europe. Carroll could have taken enough vacation time to go with me, but expressed no desire to do that kind of traveling. I was feeling pretty independent by then so I decided to go alone. I booked with a tour group meeting in London, then departing for eleven different countries within a three week time period. Our tour guide was a very charming young man from a wealthy family in Austria. He was engaged to a girl who had been recently crowned Miss Holland. She joined our tour briefly when we went to Holland; she was indeed a very beautiful girl.

I had given Carroll my itinerary, with addresses of various hotels where I would be staying and could receive mail, but I received nothing from him until I returned to London at the end of the three weeks. In the meantime, Henry, our tour guide, asked me to go dancing when we were in Rome. He took me to a marvelous place with a full orchestra and we shared a bottle of champagne. I was dancing on a cloud all evening. It was one of the most romantic evenings I had ever spent in my life. We walked from our hotel to the place where we went dancing. I remember talking mostly about my marriage and the fact that I was increasingly thinking about getting a divorce.

After becoming quite ill after eating some pizza from a street vender in Rome, I spent the next few days feeling totally miserable. We had traveled on a tour bus from Rome to Pisa. I was quite disappointed that I was unable to climb the Leaning Tower of Pisa. That night Henry brought me some tea and toast to my room since I had not been able to keep down any food since we left Rome. Being on a bus with no rest room was quite a challenge!

There was obviously an increasing attraction between myself and Henry, and I had heard nothing from Carroll since I left California, so by the time we reached Nice, Henry and I both decided to heck with the rules and finally gave in to our mutual desire to be together. This continued until it was time to leave Europe. I remember asking him what I should do about a tip since that was the proper thing to do at the end of a tour and he just asked me write to him. I did write, but never heard anything back from him. Since the letters were addressed to him at his parents' home in Austria where he lived between tours, I am guessing that his parents told him he was out of his mind to get involved with an American woman. I hope that Henry did marry Miss Holland and that they had a happy marriage. He gave me the great gift of giving me the confidence to get out of a very unhappy marriage.

I had stayed in the marriage with Carroll for ten years. We were never able to have children, which in retrospect was probably a blessing. I theorize now that he was still an employee of NSA, even though he outwardly was working for other government installations. When I applied for Social Security they could find no record of a S.S. number for him which was strange. I had to wonder if he were somehow in a hidden identity program. After our divorce he married again, twice, and according to him was very abusive to both of his wives and children. He may have been mentally abusive to me (too long ago to really remember), but the main memory of that relationship was the fact that I really didn't like him.

When we did anything socially his so-called friends would repeatedly say to him "How did an S.O.B. like you find such a nice girl?" While I took this as some kind of sorry joke, after hearing it from various sources, I began to realize that people in general didn't like him. It also became increasingly clear that we had no mutual interests. I'm not sure I had ever liked him, but sex is a powerful force and I was determined to marry him. I stuck it out for ten years mainly to prove to my parents that I was right and they were wrong. Whatever the reasons for the marriage, I would never have left Georgia if I had not married Carroll, because I loved Atlanta, and despite being apparently rather rebellious at that period of time, I deeply loved my family. I would never have had the nerve or motivation to leave Georgia if I had never met Carroll, so the marriage was no doubt meant to be and I do not regret it.

My inability to have children (which was long before the modern fertility treatments) was a strong factor in my further exploration of past lives. I dearly wanted children and wondered what terrible things I had done in a past life to make me infertile. The only answer I have ever received from psychic readings from various sources was having a family was simply not the purpose of this lifetime. However, when I had a regression myself, I came up with a different scenario, but more about that later.

As a Marriage, Family Therapist I can easily see why Carroll was abusive with his other two wives. He had a very controlling mother who often leaned on Carroll as the oldest child of three when he was growing up. The family had continual financial problems. Carroll accepted his first job with the National Security Agency (NSA) in Washington because the pay was better than any of his other offers. Then assuming that he still could not talk about his work, and no doubt was often frustrated with what he was doing, he took his suppressed anger out on his wives and children. At the time of our divorce he told me that he still loved me and did not want a divorce, but the parting was amiable. He knew that I would never have stood for physical abuse of any kind.

I last saw Carroll after he was divorced from his third wife. He drove up from his home in Arlington, Virginia to see me when I had a New York City stopover after flying back from a Rosicrucian tour I had taken to Egypt. It was then that he told me about all of the abuse. He stated that he thought his second wife was going to kill him as their fights were so violent. I really felt sorry for him but realized that divorcing him was one of the best decisions I ever made. We again parted as friends and I resumed my trip back to California. About a year later a college friend, who also had married a Georgia Tech graduate saw an announcement in the Alumni paper saying that Carroll had died about a year after our last contact. He had a very sad life, apparently almost a recluse at the end. Death was probably a relief.

Chapter 3

Past Lives with Carroll

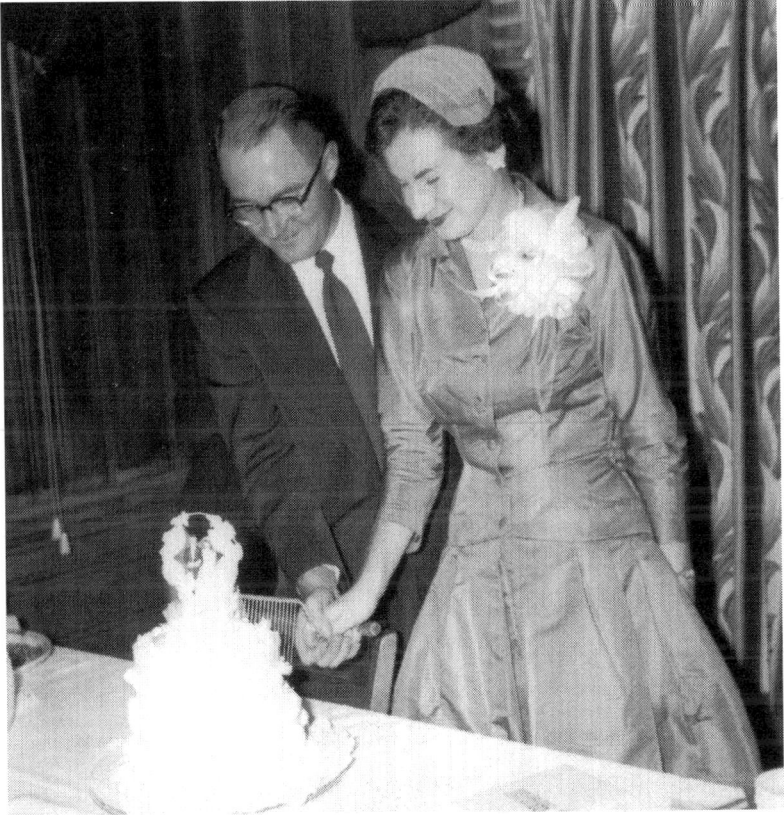

Carroll and Evelyn's wedding, 1955

In 1976 when I had a reading from Religious Research I asked about my soul relationship with Carroll. The questions are from the conductor of the reading:

Q. Has there been past life acquaintance between Evelyn and her first husband, Carroll?

A. Yes, They have been in Earth living together several times. They represent two souls from the same cosmic family, who on various occasions, have fitted well together in a given Earth learning for one soul or the other. In that sense they have been a good team together in various lifetimes. The qualities of one in expression could balance the expressed qualities of the other, and so forth.

So they have meant much to each other in the framework of incarnation for purposes of growth, and basically there is a good personal relationship soul to soul. In the present life it was very good for them to have the experience of being together. There was the strong sexual bond, and that or rather the expression of that kind of a bond is good to have as a part of the Earth experience of the soul. But they did not have much more than that, nor were they purposed to have in this life.

In other words, in this particular life, they were not the strong balancers for each other that they have been in past lives. It was time in their Earth experience to let go enough to initiate other relationships of strength for both of them. But in letting go of the Earth bond, the personality relationship, they have not on the soul level let go of their bond. That is good. That continues. That will have its place of usefulness and helpfulness in the future.

We would suggest, however, that Evelyn could accept a greater degree of letting go, a greater relinquishment. Sometimes to hold on to a relationship in friendship is very good, but at other times it serves no particular purpose and it is better completely to let the relationship lapse. We would suggest that in this specific relationship.

(End of this section of the reading.)

By the time I requested this reading I certainly thought I had let go completely of the relationship, since I was very happily married to my second husband, Wally by then. I was asking out of curiosity more than anything, and there had been no further communication with Carroll. Maybe Dr. John was tuning into what was happening with Carroll at that time. It was also true that we continued to see each other long after the divorce. He drove up from Southern CA where he was then working to meet me at Travis Air Force Base when I flew back to this country from Japan where I had taken a position as a high school counselor for a year.

He finally gave up on our relationship and married a school teacher he had met in Barstow. He made it a point to let me know when they had a child together. I presume this was to prove that our lack of children was my fault and not his! Actually I had never doubted that. I need to add that Carroll always encouraged me to continue my education. We were still married when I completed my M.A. in counseling at Sacramento State University in 1963. However, he did not come to my graduation since he had a car he was trying to sell and had an appointment with a prospective buyer. Cars were his main passion in life. He gave me a new Chevrolet without even consulting me (bought with our mutual money). It had a manual transmission, something I would have never picked.

He didn't understand why I was not exactly thrilled with this gift!

Carroll was also a patient listener when I would come home from my first teaching job in California. I had a principal who apparently decided early in the school year that, because I was from Georgia and still had a southern accent, I really was not very bright. I became good friends with the Jewish president of our PTA. Perhaps the principal thought I was also Jewish since our last names were the same, and I wondered if he had some kind of problem with Jews. At any rate, he didn't seem to be pleased with anything I did in my classroom, and gave me no support in dealing with two extremely disruptive students. I finally realized that his poor treatment of me was one of the best experiences in my life, because this resulted in my decision to go back to college and take the requirements to be a school counselor.

My subsequent principal thought I could do no wrong, asking me to teach the seventh grade gifted class after my first year teaching under his leadership. Had he been my first principal in California I would no doubt have just remained a teacher for the rest of my career; I would not have been a school counselor, nor ever gone into private practice as a therapist. I have no doubt that our lives are guided, even though it is sometimes through difficult lessons. Again, I have to thank my first husband for listening to all of my complaints and frustration through that very long year of teaching under what I thought at the time was a "principal from Hell."

I have never even asked Athor about Carroll because I have considered that a closed chapter in my life. I did not become interested in reincarnation until a number of years after my divorce from Carroll. We occasionally attended the Presbyterian Church but my spirituality was really dormant during that period of my life. I have no doubt that we both served a purpose for each other in this lifetime and very possibly will meet again in a future life. Our last meeting was amiable; therefore, I feel no karmic debt regarding Carroll. He probably incurred some heavy karma toward his other two wives and children that will need to be balanced at a future time.

Chapter 4

My Experiences in Japan

Evelyn in her office at Yamato High School, Japan

After my divorce from Carroll I spent a year in Japan as a high school counselor at Yamato High School near Tachikawa Air Force Base. This was a heady experience since there were so few Caucasian females on the base and many very interesting pilots. It was also the first step in my spiritual journey. Visiting the numerous Buddhist shrines and being exposed to many beautiful Japanese souls made me begin to question my Christian beliefs from childhood, which was that you had to accept Jesus as your savior in order to be saved and go to Heaven.

This was during the sixties and I was a liberated woman; I fell in love with three men. First, there was Jerry, an Air Force Captain, who was six years younger than I. That ended when he was transferred back to the States.

The second was Vic, a fascinating man I met on a Christmas vacation trip to Hong Kong. My feelings for Vic continued for a number of years, even though we only briefly knew each other. In fact, I finally asked about a past life relationship with him and was told that he was my wife in my last lifetime which was in England. Our plan was for him to come see me when I came back to California, but that didn't work out. A number of years later when he had flown into San Francisco (he was the manager for American Express in the Far East,) I flew from Sacramento to San Francisco to see him for part of a day. He was a former pilot and had been drinking coffee all night long while he stayed in the cockpit to talk to the pilot. His coffee high plus jet lag made it an unsatisfactory visit, but by the time I needed to leave, we both didn't want me to go. It also probably didn't help much when I told him he had been my wife in a past life! He was perhaps glad that he was never further involved with this nutty woman! Anyway, that was the end of that relationship, but I have no doubt that I loved Vic from a soul level and recognized him from our most recent past life.

My third in-depth relationship while in Japan was with a retired Air Force Colonel who was working for Air America at that time. I didn't realize it, but later learned that Air America was actually an operation of the Central Intelligence Service (CIA). Dick was the pilot of a bomber which flew on missions to Vietnam. He never talked about these flights, but he drank a great deal between assignments to Vietnam, plus he had been married four times and was thirteen years older than I. Even though we were very attracted to each other, it really was not a suitable match. When he was transferred to Thailand toward the end of my year in Japan, he asked me to fly down and join him to live there with him. I was on leave of absence from my position as a high school counselor in a school district in California and never gave his proposal any serious consideration.

Dick was an extremely interesting man. He told me that he had left his wealthy family who lived next door to the Kennedys in Boston to join the Canadian Air Force. He wanted to become a pilot and the United States was still not in World War II. As I recall I think he lied about his age in order to join the Canadian Air Force. At any rate he eventually came back to the U.S. and joined the Army Air Corp (later the Air Force,) rising to the rank of Colonel, before leaving to work for Air America. Dick had his own house on the base at Tachikawa, and loved to give parties. We had a great time together, and I was very upset when we finally had to part - Dick to Thailand and I back to California.

In retrospect, I realized that none of these men would have made a good marital partner. I was certainly not interested in getting married again anytime soon. Being romantically IN LOVE and loving someone are very different, then to throw in the factors of education, similar beliefs, similar interests etc. etc. being in a long term relationship is very serious business.

Making the decision to take a job in Japan was a huge step in my soul's growth. I was exposed to the Buddhist culture, my first experience with any faith other than Christianity, and this made me begin to question some of the Christian beliefs. The Japanese people certainly were not going to hell because they did not believe in Christ. I developed a great respect for their culture by traveling throughout most of Japan, but mainly through my relationships with the Japanese people. As an example, my Japanese secretary was not only highly efficient but became a good friend. We corresponded many years after I left Japan.

Although I lived on base, another teacher and I went into Tokyo quite frequently. Darlene, my friend, was an extrovert who talked to any and every one, so we met lots of interesting people. She somehow met a man who turned out to be the President of Air India. He had an apartment in Tokyo and invited us to come to one of his many parties. I don't remember the details, but one of his friends informed Darlene that he really liked me and had decided he wanted to marry me. I was astonished because I hardly knew him, and later decided that maybe I was to be "one" of his wives, since very possibly he had other wives. Whatever the situation, Darlene and I never went back to any of his parties!

I was to gain a great deal of confidence in myself through living in a foreign country, having arrived knowing no one, but had many lasting friendships by the time I came back to California.

I still knew nothing about past lives, extraterrestrials, etc., but I certainly learned that there are many good people who are Buddhists.

After returning to the US, I was very busy with my new assignment as the freshman counselor at a high school that was just opening. As for the dating scene, all the men I met at various single functions were most unappealing, a huge contrast from those I had known in Japan. Since I was basically an empathetic person, I had great difficulty turning down the few men who seemed very interested in me. I can't understand how women can sometimes be so rude and downright cruel in the dating game. I could never do that. One of my worst experiences was when a man, whom I had actually only dated a few times, got down on his knees and proposed to me. I was astounded and had no idea how to respond. I don't recall exactly what I said but I tried to turn him down as gently as possible since he was an extremely nice man, but I hardly knew him.

Toi was a widower. His children were grown, and I'm sure he was quite lonely, a situation that I can certainly relate to at this point in my life. Toi was of Japanese descent, was a retired engineer, and I surmise attracted to me mainly because I had spent a year in Japan and genuinely admired the Japanese culture. He eventually married a retired teacher; I was happy to hear that he had found someone else.

Chapter 5

Wally, My Geologist Husband

Wally, 1972

I met Wally, my second husband, right before Christmas in 1968. He was an engineering geologist with the California Department of Water Resources. He had first dated a friend of mine, a school psychologist. He later told me that he was hesitant to ask me out because he felt he was too old for me (almost eleven years my senior), but our relationship developed very fast after a few dates and we were married within a year. He had been working in the Sacramento department downtown when we first met, but by the time we were married he had been transferred to Palmdale, California to work on the state aqueduct system to deliver water to Southern California.

Wally resented this transfer very much since his mother and two daughters from a former marriage lived in Sacramento. In addition, I had a job I loved and was having difficulty finding a new position in the schools in the Palmdale area. We were married in February over a holiday weekend so spent the rest of the school year meeting halfway in Fresno. I finally took a leave of absence thinking that maybe Wally would soon be transferred back to Sacramento. That didn't happen; our stay in Palmdale turned out to be seven years.

After three years Wally was transferred to an office in downtown Los Angeles, but he refused to move there since once again I had a job I really liked and we had bought a home in Palmdale. Wally hated the two hour commute each way, as well as his job. He began drinking quite heavily, became depressed, almost suicidal at times. Despite my protest, sometimes he would go walking with our dog in the desert at night with a gun. He said the gun was to kill rattlesnakes, but I wasn't at all sure he would come home.

I came from a home where my family would have a small glass of wine on New Year's Eve, but that was the extent of our consumption of alcohol. No doubt my friend Dick, in Japan, was an alcoholic. There was a great deal of alcohol abuse at Tachikawa, but I had very little personal experience with substance abuse. However, Wally and I were still very much in love, and in retrospect, I guess I chose to just ignore the problem. In fact, during the first few years of our marriage, I kept wondering how I could be so lucky to have such a loving, wonderful husband. Until his transfer to L.A. we were never apart, except one weekend that I attended a workshop up in the mountains, but missed Wally so much that I really did not enjoy it.

During this period I began to wonder about a lot of things; the desert seems to have an effect of spiritual awakening and self-examination. I had grown up in the Presbyterian Church. My grandfather was an elder in the church, and I had two uncles who were Presbyterian ministers. When I visited my grandparents it was tradition to read a passage from the Bible before going to bed at night.

In Palmdale I joined the local Presbyterian Church, but really began questioning their beliefs after observing the terrible treatment of students by a teacher at my school who was one of the leaders of the church. Apparently she didn't live by her so-called beliefs. Her students would regularly come into my office crying because of her mental and sometimes even physical abuse of them. Of course, by then, I had also spent a year in Japan where I met many devout, wonderful people who were Buddhists.

I decided to attend the Church of Religious Science, and liked what they taught, but also explored further by attending some Eckankar classes. I studied Transcendental Meditation, and finally became a member of the Rosicrucians, attending several large conferences in Los Angeles.

I can't say exactly when I became interested in reincarnation, but I do remember it was during this period in Palmdale. I was still wondering why I could not have children, although Wally was really not interested in having more children. Probably another factor was my counseling work at an elementary school. I had been working with high school students prior to this, but now I was seeing kindergarten through sixth grade students and began to wonder why so many of these children were in extremely dysfunctional families, and in such abject poverty from birth. It didn't fit in with what I had learned through traditional Christian religion.

Actually, the concept of reincarnation was something new to me, but it began to make a great deal of sense. Now my belief is that we choose our birth parents, so there were either karmic reasons why these children had picked certain parents, or they were born into a family to help the parents, and/or siblings. My relationship with Wally was certainly karmic, having had numerous incarnations where we played both the negative and the positive role. We needed to be together again to balance out the relationship. I feel we succeeded, although during our almost twenty-five years of marriage until his transition in 1994, it was certainly a bumpy road!

Wally was eventually transferred back to the Sacramento office, but once again I had a job in Palmdale that I loved. My work as a home school coordinator in an elementary school was quite difficult. In addition to counseling, it required home visits in remote areas where I often was confronted with big vicious dogs. I had to plan field trips for Title I students and parents to go on bus trips to various places for so-called cultural enrichment. The goal was to raise IQ scores; this required me to test the students before and after the series of field trips. Unfortunately the scores did not have a statistically significant increase, but it did improve attendance and attitude toward school.

At any rate, I jumped at the chance to interview for a position at the local middle school in Palmdale. I was delighted to be chosen for the job and after spending the first few years trying to convince everyone that it was a worthwhile idea to have a counselor; I relaxed and really enjoyed my work. Middle school students were a huge challenge, but you could talk to them much as you would an adult, and I found my work very rewarding.

When Wally returned to Sacramento, I stayed in Palmdale to sell our home and finish the school year. We returned to commuting to be together every two weeks, although this time it was flying out of Burbank, except for holiday vacations when I drove all the way back up the valley. I had been seeing some clients for Marriage, Family Counseling at Antelope Valley Family Services, but it never occurred to me to do that kind of work fulltime, since the schools had been my career for many years. At that time my old district was not hiring counselors and my leave of absence had run out.

When we finally decided we couldn't handle the commuting bit anymore I decided to take another leave of absence from my job in Palmdale, and moved back to Sacramento without a job. I was unemployed for a year, but took that time to go back to Sacramento State University where I had received my M.A. in counseling. While there I took courses in special education, since I was told that was where the jobs were. Indeed I did finally get a job as a halftime counselor and halftime resource specialist working with special education students. After again becoming a full time counselor, I remained in that position for seven years and retired from the schools at age 55.

Even though I loved working with children again, it was an extremely difficult job. To survive, I decided to get my doctorate in psychology and go into private practice as soon as I reached minimum retirement age. My plan was to write my dissertation on research into past lives, but my advisor stated emphatically that there was no such thing as past lives. My struggle with his philosophy went on for some time until I finally decided I would never earn a Ph.D. unless I did it his way. That was a good decision because later many clients came to see me because of my highly academic background that gave validity to my work which was mainly past life regression therapy. Later I discovered Athor, and then my life started going in a different direction.

After my retirement, Wally and I designed a large office complex which was added on to our house in Rocklin. Not many years after Wally had been transferred back to the Sacramento area, his physical problems accelerated to the point he was forced to retire. He had constant pain from his back problems that resulted from some falls during his geology work. He still resented all of his job transfers by the state, which he attributed to his supervisor who seemed to really hate him. This was strange, because Wally was a very likeable person, with many friends. However, this particular man seemed to be really out to get him, which made no rational sense. I am now sure they must have had an extremely negative past life connection.

Due to Wally's depression and anger toward the state, we began to grow apart, but our main problem was my new belief system. He used to tell me that I was not the same person as the woman he married, and he was quite right. Once one begins on a true spiritual path one changes, and I was frustrated continually by his inability to accept any of my beliefs. Although he had gone to church with me occasionally, he didn't have any belief in God, and stated that when we die that is the end of it. I thought this was sad, but later when I requested an Off-Earth life reading for Wally this was explained. He genuinely wanted to have a spiritual belief system but even before he knew me, various people had tried to change his views with no success. If it couldn't be explained by science then it had no validity.

I wish Wally could have lived long enough to see that science and spirituality are finally beginning to merge together. On the other hand he realized that my work was important to me and did a great deal to plan my office addition. He also supported my giving workshops and talks about my work, along with encouraging me to write *From Sirius to Earth*. Wally was very funny, always telling corny jokes and drawing cute little pictures on cards he gave to me. He had been totally dedicated to his work as a geologist, being one of the pioneers for the California State Water Project. His desire had been to work until at least age 65, but was forced to retire much earlier, which added to his grievance with the state.

Wally filed a lawsuit against the state, but by the time it was finally settled most of the money went to doctors and attorneys. It took an emotional toll on both of us, and was certainly not worth it. Wally was diagnosed with acute leukemia only a few months before he made his transition. I was proud of him during his last year because he finally made the decision to stop drinking, quitting cold turkey. I can't be sure that there was any correlation with his decision to become sober, but I was so distressed over his drinking that I made an appointment with Dr. William Baldwin, who specialized in spiritual de-possession. By then I knew this could be the reason some people become alcoholics.

Dr. Baldwin had gotten into his line of work due to his own experience as an alcoholic, and was considered an expert in this area. It was a fascinating session. I really did not feel hypnotized, but told a story about Wally working in the psychiatric unit of a Naval Hospital and finding a patient who had committed suicide by hanging himself. The patient had been possessed by the spirit that left a Japanese soldier during one of the battles during World War II. This apparently was a very angry spirit which became Earthbound, and somehow attached to the patient. During the time Wally was in the Service he was classified as a Pharmacist Mate (the Navy term for Medic).Perhaps Wally's patient and this Japanese soldier had been in a battle together. This spirit was released when the patient died and attached to Wally. Dr. Baldwin then proceeded to talk the spirit into going into the Light and leaving the Earth plane.

When I told Wally this story he was amazed and seemed to feel that it could be true, since he had indeed found a patient who had hanged himself while he was serving his time at the Naval Hospital. His mother had told me repeatedly that Wally never drank until he joined the Service; however, I thought that was probably true of many young men who joined the Service during wartime. It was much later when I learned about earthbound spirits attaching to people who drink and consequently develop holes in their auras.

After his last long bout in the hospital following a severe staph infection of the bone, he was told that this could be the result of his heavy drinking, and that really scared him. Even then he did not stop drinking once he had recuperated somewhat from the foot infection. He never thought of himself as an alcoholic, therefore, had no interest in attending AA meetings or going into any kind of rehab program.

Unfortunately his primary doctor at Kaiser Permanente in Sacramento never discussed his drinking problem, even after I went to one of Wally's appointments with him and asked the doctor to urge Wally to stop drinking. I only realized the extent of his problem, however, after he had died. I was clearing out a rented storage locker and discovered dozens of liquor bottles that I presume he was hiding from me. It was then that I realized I should have done some intervention, but Wally was so unhappy that, in a way, I think he was trying to kill himself at a subconscious level.

This brings me to all of the past life information which has helped me understand Wally. Knowing what I did about his past life background gave me great insight into what was going on with him at a soul level. During my Ph.D. program I was required to have 30 hours of therapy (required of all doctoral candidates). I quickly ran out of things to discuss with my psychologist except for the problems in my marriage, therefore, the remaining sessions were all with both me and Wally. At the end the psychologist expressed the concern that he had little hope for the marriage to survive. All along Wally had clung to me tenaciously, totally opposed to a divorce. I knew that I still loved him on a deep soul level, but I seriously doubt we would have stayed together until his transition without my understanding of Wally's soul pattern.

Chapter 6

Past Lives of Evelyn and Wally

On and Off-Earth

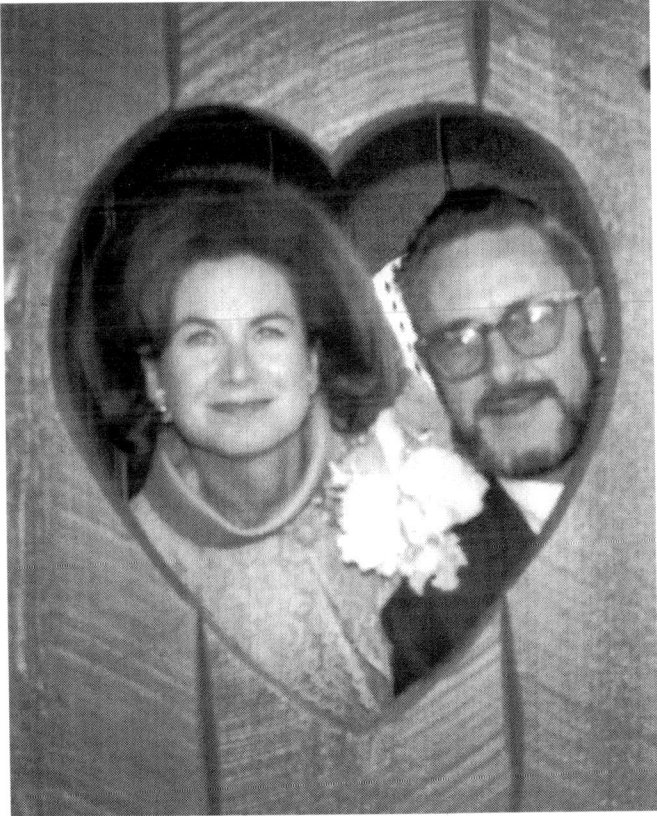

Evelyn and Wally - Wedding Chapel at Rough and Ready, CA
1970

Despite Wally's excessive abuse of alcohol, our marital problems did not really start until after the move back to the Sacramento area and finally Wally's forced retirement in 1978. By then I had already established a firm belief in reincarnation. I did not know Athor yet, but after reading a book about the work of Dr. Franklin Loehr I requested a reading from him about Wally. I had earlier had two readings about myself which seemed to ring true, and had read a number of books published by his organization, Religious Research, in Grand Island, Florida. Therefore, I felt I could probably trust the information coming from his spirit guide, Dr. John Christopher Daniel. It was my hope that a reading would give me a spiritual understanding of why I was with Wally, and help me make a wise decision regarding whether we should stay together.

When Dr. John gave readings he would give the soul age in five stages such as very young, young, around the mid-point, well along, or an old soul. His readings also stated whether the person was from the male or female portion of the soul based on the theory that the soul is both male and female from its inception, but the two halves break apart and go through their own evolution. The other half is considered the twin soul. Both may incarnate on Earth at the same time, but often in different parts of the world, or the other half of the soul may be in a different dimension or on another planet. It is really seldom that the two halves meet while in an Earth incarnation. If they do meet, it is not necessarily wonderful bliss the way many may think because the energies are so intense. Each has had his/her own evolutionary path which may not be compatible with the other for Earth living.

To quote from the Religious Research Introduction: "If you have lived even once before, you never will understand yourself or anyone else in terms of one lifetime only. Forces from past lives join with our present life personality forces (heredity, environment, childhood upbringing, our personal decisions, etc.) to make us what we are and what we are becoming. We live many lifetimes; each life has some particular purpose (perhaps several purposes), and to know this element of purpose can be the most important factor of all." I now believe that to have a fuller understanding of one's soul you need to also know about what happened between the creation of the soul and the beginning incarnations on Earth.

The first information about Wally came from a reading I had requested from Religious Research for myself in 1976. We were still very much in love and I was frustrated by our continued separation due to our job situations.

Q: Has there been past life acquaintance between Evelyn and Wallace?
A: Yes. They have been together a number of times as cosmic family members, but they have not been in Earth living together now for a number of lifetimes. The fact that their paths on Earth separated over a period of Earth time and now have come together again with the present life, gives the two souls a special gladness at being together in Earth living once again. The fact that they would be together in this lifetime was a strong element giving anticipation and gladness as the two souls prepared for this lifetime, and led to a soul recognition on the part of each of them which brought the two personalities together rather quickly.

The last time they were incarnated together was as husband and wife, in a relationship in which their roles as father and mother were a major factor; and this was stressed. This was a lifetime in the 500's A.D. It was a lifetime in China. The present Wally soul was the husband, she was the wife. They had thirteen children. As we say, the role of parents was major to both souls in that lifetime. The personalities and the personality life were focused upon that.

Their marriage as young people, quite young, in their early teens, was the marriage of two prominent families in the community. It united two families, it united two fortunes. So there were adequate resources for having the large family. As we say, the two souls were very happy in the father-mother role. They never tired of it. A new child was a great joy to them.

They enjoyed all of their children at every age, not just in babyhood. So while they were rejoicing in the advent of a new little one into their home, they were also rejoicing in the growth and maturing of the eldest child, and everyone in between. That was the most recent Earth life which, as you can see, wasn't very recent.

I'm glad I was a good parent then, but frankly cannot imagine having 13 children; however, that was the way it worked in many cultures back in those days.

Q: Will these two cosmic family members come together again in future lives?
A: Yes.

The reading I requested specifically for Wally was not until five years later in 1981 after our problems were becoming more apparent. I had begun my doctoral program and was beginning to wonder if our marriage would survive.

Dr. John begins the reading with the following:

The most basic thing I can say possibly, the most helpful perhaps, is the soul identification. Wallace, although a very good Earth man, is an incarnation from the feminine half of his whole soul and is a fairly young soul. He is in the second of the five states into which, for sake of convenience, I have divided the soul's progression through incarnations and through soulhood. He is nearing the end of that second stage and in another several incarnations should enter the "around-the-midpoint" state wherein, as with the famous "Bell curve," most of the phenomena of incarnations and soulhood take place. At present he has had probably 15 to 19 significant incarnations, depending on what the reader would mean by "significant."

This is not the first masculine incarnation by any means, but this is one into which certain requirements have been introduced, which are somewhat new for this soul, new in degree, let us say. Actually he probably has had a rather difficult lifetime in a number of areas because of one basic difficulty, the soul feeling a bit inept at masculine living, and actually being certainly not as expert at it as the soul will be when it has another 10 or 20 masculine incarnations behind it. Now this is a matter of attitude as well as events, but let us let it rest at this point and I will return to this later in his Reading with some possible suggestions. Well, let us say with some suggestions for possible use and helpfulness in his living, if he chooses.

Q: What is his soul relationship with his wife, Evelyn? (Even though I had asked about this before, I wanted to see if he came up with the same information, since I always have a skeptical mind).
A: She is a cosmic family member, and the two of them are very meaningfully and purposefully and pre-planned together in this life (old information,) but they may not end their lifetime together (new information). That is, I see a cloud on that relationship at present, and this is a very serious matter and one wherein perhaps I can bring particular helpfulness. His wife is really verging into what we would call an old soul, in the fourth stage of "well along", and she has her own purposes, her own growth in this life, and that pattern and that growth will be maintained and he must not infringe upon it; or if he does, as he has and somewhat is, she must maintain her own integrity. In other words, just to be with him is not the only purpose in her life, and he would not wish it to be so. But it is one of the major factors in the lives of both of them, and on the soul level they understood the general areas of growth to be accomplished by each in these incarnations, and they were glad to assist each other and to take their growing and their problems together, for all growing has certain problems. It is a progression

from masteries attained to new masteries, the attainment of more understanding and control of life.

They have been together a number of times, but not really recently. (He then cites the lifetime in China again.) That was what I would call a "grace of God lifetime", in which masculine qualities which had not yet been earned by effort and experiences were bestowed upon the then incarnation of the Wallace soul. Life-wise, the demands were less. There was not a real problem in earning a livelihood for that husband and father as there were ample family resources at their disposal. Yes, he worked, but he worked within an already established family framework, and the demands were not the same as going out upon his own into the world with a job. That was really a very lovely lifetime (again gives details that were given in the first reading five years ago).

I next go back to the 300s A.D. I find the then incarnation of the Wallace soul was in the feminine expression. The then incarnation of the Evelyn soul was in the masculine as a 2-year older brother. The Cosmic Family bond made them close together, and also the "pull of the future" brought a great deal of closeness to them in preparation for the 500's lifetime which was to come, which already had been pretty well structured in the pattern.

To assist in this preparatory nature, this life also was in China. The family into which they were born, was not as well endowed with material position and resources, was not as affluent. The father was a merchant and really provided very well for his family in putting the family into perhaps the top quartile economically, so there was not want. They enjoyed each other in the living out of the pattern of that lifetime.

I find them next in the 200s B.C. Here they are brothers, and the then incarnation of the Wallace soul is an older brother by slightly under a year. This is in Africa in one of the Black tribes there; it is a tribe that is advanced both in its culture and in its genetic endowment. The people have a good level of intelligence. Had they had the cultural institutions of even the present day they would have made good use of them and they could have made good citizens of even your American economy and society of the 20th century. The tribe, as would be expected from one culturally advanced, had enough size, enough political organizations of strength, that it was free from marauders and had a sufficiently productive economy so that they could become relatively cultured.

The two boys were encouraged to find out what the world was like, and the younger soul was allowed to be the older brother quite purposefully so that he would not feel that the younger brother was leading and guiding him. It was wanted that the younger soul have a certain confidence and be put in the position of being the older brother. However, the younger brother, of course, had more soul experience with Earth, and so in the deep subconscious had a greater knowledge of what to do. The older brother, at such a time as he was in doubt, would let the younger brother quietly sort of take the lead or make a suggestion and thus the two were fine brothers all through that life. They were strong and healthy. They

44

married and had good families. They were good productive members of the society, although they were not in the leadership council nor did they aspire to be. But they made a good life in that pattern.

I go back now to the early 9th century about 890 B.C. This is the first significant Earth life in the feminine expression, the present wife as father. The sponsor soul was present in the mother (very young souls have a sponsor soul to help them adjust to Earth living). This was in Egypt, near the Mediterranean, and life had acquired certain amenities: philosophy, knowledge, and education, although education was not so much in established schools as in the temples which served many functions then. (He goes into a long discussion about the role of the temples at that time which does not seem relevant to this book.)

This was not the first time this soul had "touched down" into Earth; the soul will often come into several proto-personalities before it actually does put foot down upon Earth and stay (for instance, infant deaths). This soul did not die in infancy (that had occurred before, I believe) and did not die at puberty. The general ease of the society and the fact that both parents were really older souls smoothed out the transition from girlhood to womanhood, which is too much of a transition for many beginning souls, and so this one came into the teens but did not experience marriage. Marriage was being seriously contemplated by the parent, but by the 16th birthday the person was removed. It was done from the spirit side and as so many of the unexplained things of Earth life are done; many of the puzzles and questions of Earth really have their answers on the spirit side. So the girl rather wasted away within a week and died. Both parents on the soul level were knowledgeable, and the spirit side of life was able to get through to them with a certain solace and they understood at a deep level. They viewed the transition to a larger and better sphere of life, which it really was.

Q: Will they have a future together?

A: Yes, although it may be delayed, depending upon what he understands and values their relationship. His Council is quite concerned at this point. There are three of his Council of Guides and Teachers present and one from the Supervisory Council, and then there is a certain Light figure here as well which does not identify itself. They tell me the person has gotten somewhat out of control. Now were the Wallace soul older, more experienced, it could have held its personhood in control better. But this person is allowed its own understandings, its own consciousness, and somewhat its own ego to get out of control and it may come to some rather difficult and quite unpleasant experiences.

Q: There are quite a few problems in the marriage relationship. They are very different and there are many daily living type conflicts.

A: The husband is insisting on his own way. This is a young feminine soul, uncertain of itself in masculine expression and it translates in this case, as very often, into a masculine pressure for its own way and insistence that it is right. If it were truly confident, it would be a more child-like attitude, more of a willingness to learn. Unless there is a willingness to

46

learn, an admission that he does not have full knowledge, a non-insistence upon asserting his understanding as being the necessary truth in his household and in his life and in his relationships; unless he drops his resistance to further learning - the marriage and many other things he holds dear to life are very much jeopardized. His wife must not violate the basic integrity of her being and her purpose and her growth in this life simply to meet restrictions that he established and upon which he insists. If Wallace insists on his understandings as reality, life will simply bring him abrasive contact with the real reality. Hopefully he will learn before his transition. After the transition into the other stage he will see the reality of the spiritual elements of life because he will be in a non-physical plane, but hopefully for his own comfort he will learn before his transition.

Q: All of this would probably explain why he has so many job-related problems and would this also affect his physical problems?

A: What is his work?

Q: His former work was in geology, but right now he is retired from government work.

A: This was a courageous choice. That soul is not cowardly. A fairly young soul operating in its non-native valence with less courage could have chosen a simpler life, but this soul with a great deal of courage chose to know Earth, as it were, and to in a sense take mastery of Earth, to live the vigorous life of that profession. This had quite a lot of insight. The soul realized this was an area in which growth was to be attained and it said, "Give me a good measure of growth to be attained in this life". We congratulate him upon that.

Q: What about his physical problems?

A: The ineptitude of any person in a new situation is a factor. A person attempting the first time to take apart and put together an automotive engine will injure himself, and the engine! It might take a lot of time and experience, and much frustration with it. Experience makes for a greater ease and ability, and a lack of experience does make everything more difficult. Here is an attitude as we find often in a young soul that "I will be so good at this," or "I must not let anybody find out that I am a young soul and rather new at this"...the toll it takes is compounded. It's not only inexperience but it is really an attitude which hurts and exacts a further toll, laying a further burden upon one.

Q: Evelyn's questions all revolved around why they are together and whether or not they should stay together.

A: Well, she should not stay with him if he becomes too burdensome, if he would destroy the integrity of her beingness or limit too much the purpose of her incarnation. One of the purposes is to be supportive of him but it is not the only purpose and it is not the chief purpose. She serves God, not man. He will be better when he does too.

The reader will note that the reading did not address Wally's alcoholism directly because I didn't ask about that. However, one can surmise that a fairly young soul in its non-native gender could certainly resort to drinking when things became just too difficult to handle. There will be more about this when we get into the Athor reading about Wally's Off-Earth origins.

I completed my Ph.D. in 1983, and retired from the school system in 1987. My marriage continued to be difficult, but I survived by being away from home a great deal. I was the State Relations Chairman for the California Counselors Association. This involved a Board Meeting once a month, with periodic meetings with all the Officers and various chairmen of the Association. Along with this I was elected a Board member of the Association of Past Life Therapy (now International Association of Regression Therapies,) eventually being elected Vice-President. Being on the Board was time consuming since there were many Board meetings and Conferences to attend. I found that being the Vice-President was quite demanding, being in charge of planning all the conferences and introducing the speakers at the conferences. When the President decided to run for another term and wanted me to continue as Vice-President, I declined which of course meant I would never be President, but I became reconciled to that.

These various functions met all over the state of California, most of the meetings and conferences being in Southern CA. I'm sure my being away from home so much was difficult for Wally, particularly since, with my work schedule, he was the one solely responsible for taking care of our one acre yard in Rocklin.

When I retired from the schools and wanted to go into private practice, Wally was a great help in the building of my office addition onto our house. In his own way he was always very proud of me for everything I did. He often gave me many metaphysical type gifts, such as a small projector device that cast rainbows on the ceiling of my office, and crystals which he knew I loved. However, he continued to have no belief in life after death, reincarnation, UFOs, or any of the things that were part of my way of life.

Finally, after Rose/Athor came to me for counseling and subsequently started doing readings for clients, I began asking her questions about our relationship. Dr. Franklin Loehr, the trance channel for Dr. John, had made his transition and was no longer available for me to seek guidance. All along, of course, I felt I was following my own inner guidance since I had decided to stay with Wally. However, it has been my mission to search for soul understanding, and I wanted to know what may have happened to Wally's soul before it started incarnations here on Earth, something that perhaps would explain his inability to be open to anything spiritual. The reading by Athor gave me tremendous insight into his soul's resistance to any kind of enlightenment.

This reading was requested January 4, 1992, and continued on January 28, 1992. Please keep an open mind because much of this material is downright bizarre to our earthly minds; but it is all part of the on-going evolutionary process. I simply ask you to consider all of this as possibilities

Athor: There is a ball of light which splits into two parts, much as your nucleus or an egg which begins to divide. Of the two, the one light goes in an upward spiral, and the other has gone into a lower rate of frequency. First of all, this seems to indicate that this is not the complete (I am not sure 'soul' is the correct word, but that's all I get right now) soul. There is another aspect to this soul.

Evelyn: The other aspect is residing in the Light?

Athor: Yes. When the (lower frequency) Light comes forth it is seen that it impacts upon a body in space, perhaps a planet; but there is no vegetation as such. As the Light hits, it scatters all over. It takes seed within the surface of this body. We see plant-like vegetation that sprouts forth, but this is not Earth-type vegetation. It has a rudimentary type of consciousness different from your Earth plants. There is more of a sentience about its senses, its feeling nature. They move very fluidly about here and there.

There is one in particular, one of these plant-like creatures that entwines itself around another and the two are entwined here. It's like there's a tremendous thrust in this plant-like being to merge, to meld, to unite and to come together. (Athor later explains that this was an attempt to reunite with the higher essence of the soul.) It seems like in the original splitting it is already trying to merge and unite with this other plant. It has almost a stranglehold on it; because of its rudimentary consciousness it does not understand anything else. Because of this twining effect it manages to uproot itself. It jumps off the surface and kind of floats away. (Athor sees pictures much like a movie and attempts to interpret what she sees.)

Then we have a small ball of Light from the other part of this ball of Light which had split, and it is sending forth a beam of Light toward this body we have just viewed. How odd! It produces something like a healing, because it was almost a violent act in the twining and uprooting described. We see that there is still the rudimentary consciousness in the plant life which is floating out there, but it is floating in darkness. It is just kind of orbiting around a planetary body. The consciousness that is seen finally leaves the form that is orbiting, as we see a small pinpoint of Light disengaging from that plant life.

So we have a rather complicated life form. Now we are following this pinpoint of Light. It searches; it seems to be traveling. It finds a planetary body which has a red sun circling around it. The sun is not nearly as large as our sun in this galactic system. The Light seeks to enter the sun, but is repelled. It seems lost. That was a Light source it tried to merge with, but it was not possible to merge with the sun. It next came on the surface of that planet. It took on a shape which is amorphous, and a grayish blue. It had some shape, but it constantly changed its shape. It was fluidic, more like plasma, so it's kind of just moving, propelling itself over the surface of this planet. It kind of looks like a stingray, but it's much more fluidic in motion; however, it had the same kind of motion as a stingray.

As it moves over that planet, it kind of sucks up certain nutrients and energies from the planet, and it seems to have many mouths or areas from which it can absorb energies and substance. Then it moves out into space. There doesn't seem to be any consciousness which is even understood in humans at this time. There is not a sense of self-awareness. There's rather an instinctive seeking and reaching and exploring without self-consciousness behind it. It's just kind of going here and there.

As it moves out into space, energy hits it mid-center − poosh -- and the form is dissipated. Once again we have the little ball of Light. This one seems to just bounce around again, and it spends a considerable amount of time just bouncing around, not having enough consciousness to have awareness of what it is seeing. It is just observing, but there is no processing of this.

It is seen that it comes forth on the planet where Evelyn came from, where she had many existences. It first takes the form of a crystal formation, and that is partly where his geological interests stem from. It took the form of one of these formations. These were not intelligent formations as were known on Earth, as your crystals on Earth are not intelligent as humans understand intelligence. But there is a similarity, although there was not as much density in these formations. This one was there for a period of time. It chose to give off a red-type of color midst a sea of crystals. It was the only one that gave off this ray of color.

Someone or something experimented, and an energy or ray was directed at this crystal, and it began to give off this Light. As it began to radiate this color, it began to heat up and finally the crystal formation was no more. There was someone who was experimenting to just find out what would happen.

Evelyn: Did I have any direct contact with this crystal?

Athor: I hear, yes.

Evelyn: Was I experimenting?

Athor: I hear, yes. One moment please. There was a very different type of consciousness here. We are looking at this garden of crystals, but the Beings (crystals) had freedom of movement, and they could

53

really go anywhere; so it wasn't just your garden of crystals. For some reason, you just happened to be there at this time, and picked this crystal. Something about the shape piqued your curiosity; so this is what is going on here.

The Being took some other non-descriptive forms again, and then it came forth as your pet. It is seen again as a plasma-like substance, but there is more development. The Beings did not have the consciousness of your species; they were like the animal kingdom would be to humans on Earth. There was a loving feeling, a bond of some type of trust that we feel between the two species we are viewing. Some of your species just tolerated these. Some experimented on them, and some of them trained them or domesticated them. There was some kind of experiment, but at some point, there was a feeling of trust that was established, and a feeling of good will, although almost instinctive on your part. That, of course, was one of the times that the Wally soul had a vague memory of adoration in which there was advancement in the species.

Sometime afterward, the Being came into a system where they were more humanoid in appearance. It appears similar in appearance to the Beings in Whitley Strieber's *Communion*. They were somewhat short, but had large heads and large eyes. They also had a sub-classification of species which were more lizard-like, and they were like a hybrid species which evidently they had collected from some other system. They didn't actually produce them there; they had manufactured them elsewhere, but they had help. So they had taken these reptilian creatures back with them, and this one looks quite similar to an alligator, but it has a strange way it moves –not so much with legs. It exerts a pressure from the abdominal area and just sort of hops from place to place. That's the method of propelling the body.

Evelyn: So the Wally soul is the reptilian type, not the *Communion* type?

Athor: Yes. But there are some Beings that are viewing it – watching it to see how they can improve on the species. It is of a denser substance than these Beings. One of these Beings is doing some type of telepathic exchange with this creature (Wally.) What seems to occur is that Being trades places with the consciousness of the reptilian Being. It has traded places with this reptilian form, and the other one has entered the upright Being's form. It is a horrible experiment, because both suffer tremendously. The one (Wally soul) not being ready for this jump in frequency to a much higher frequency, and the other for the opposite reason.

The Wally consciousness is extremely frightened. It's just in a state of panic because, in comparison to the rate of frequency of this embodiment, and this Being; it is just in pure darkness in terms of rates of frequencies. It sees itself as darkness, but isn't aware of the dichotomy, the brightness of the Light. The higher frequency brings out the slower frequency to the nth degree. It exposes it. So the Being feels it is filled with darkness. It sees itself as a void, as a pit. That memory is very, very strong in the consciousness of this Being. And that is where the fear of the Light, the most horrendous strong panic comes from, because of this experimentation. The Light Body had not evolved to any degree of self-consciousness as a Light Body, that is, and aspect of the soul. These Beings were highly advanced in many ways, but they were unaware of this factor.

In many other Athor readings we discovered numerous experiments which had gone wrong, but left an impact on the soul that carried over into Earth incarnations.

Evelyn: So in a sense this was a Soul Exchange?
Athor: Yes.
Evelyn: Did this take place in another galaxy?
Athor: Yes. It was somewhat similar to this galactic system, but more advanced technology.
Evelyn: What happened to the Wally soul then?
Athor: It went into a state of spiritual shock, you might say. It had a spiritual nervous breakdown, if such a thing is possible. It had a consciousness breakdown. It's like it fried all the circuits of the rudimentary consciousness which were present. It did not extinguish the soul Light, but the consciousness was greatly damaged. Had it been allowed to evolve in a more natural sequence and had not been tampered with, it would not have this deep rooted memory of this – it correlates the Light with annihilation. (Dr. John repeatedly had cautioned me to not push Wally; let him evolve at his own rate.) As indeed, in a sense, it did occur on that level, and we see that the Being left the form of the *Communion* type-looking Being, and

the dark remnant dropped off. Then we have the little ball of Light again.

It goes through this planetary body, then up through space and hits a dimensional wall, and it stops its travel. Since it was still only a ball of Light, it didn't have any consciousness as humans know it. It had no comprehension of ...okay; it got stopped here, so it tried going elsewhere but was stopped again. Pretty soon it found itself to be in the center of this force field which became smaller and smaller.

This ball was trying desperately to move, and the space in which it could move got narrower and narrower until there was a tremendous pressure. It was like being inside a vise. It became clothed with other energies, other frequencies which did not come from within itself. It's like wherever these frequencies originated from, they stopped this Light. They solidified it and froze it in time and space, I hear. There was this rudimentary awareness of a panic of not having any direction in which to go. This again goes together with the Soul Exchange experience. That adds to the panic. The two memories combined are very, very strong. When the pressure reaches a certain point, there is a collapsing of the energies – perhaps it is a dimensional shift. She then begins to go into a number of Earth lives.

This very involved description of Wally's soul before he came into a physical incarnation here on Earth is quite difficult for most people to understand; but having heard many readings which involved trauma prior to coming to Earth, I was not as shocked as much as many of my readers may be. It helped me a great deal to understand Wally's soul pattern and why it was so difficult for him to accept anything spiritual. Within two years after this reading Wally's soul made its transition. Up until the time he lapsed into a coma, he was terrified of dying. To him, it was a void, just darkness. Because of this reading I knew how very difficult it would be for him to leave the Earth plane and go back into a spiritual realm. I very much feared he would become Earth-bound. I could sense his presence for a number of weeks.

Finally, with Athor's help we were able to send him into The Light. I knew exactly when he left, because one night I woke up terrified. I had never been afraid to stay alone, so this feeling was totally irrational for no apparent reason. Instinctively, I reached up and turned on a light over the bed. Instantly the fear was gone and I felt an overwhelming sense of peace. I was so happy for Wally that he could move on. Much later I asked Athor about his progress on the other side. He had been through so much trauma that he spent some time in something akin to a hospital where much healing took place. Then he progressed to the point where he was doing research in a "library," where he was finding that there was much validity to my beliefs. I would like to think that his soul took a large step forward in its evolutionary path as the result of our almost 25 years together.

The various lifetimes here on Earth given in Wally's Athor reading were usually ones filled with further trauma. Dr. John gave the more peaceful lifetimes, but since I was a therapist and suggested Athor readings to unearth the root cause of problems, the readings she gave were usually far from peaceful. Wally's strong interest in geology was in part because the Earth was apparently his home planet, the first time he began to have conscious awareness. One very long description was about his being in an earthquake which killed his entire clan when they went into their cave for the night. He was the last one in, so escaped, but was unable to remove all the rocks that blocked the entrance to the cave. This was one of his early lives as a male. His constant need to save things and be prepared for a cataclysmic event was related to the earthquake lifetime. He also had many cycles when he was engaged in war-type activities. There was a great deal, on both sides, of brutalization which occurred to physical bodies.

Wally always seemed to have a love/hate relationship with his mother. In another lifetime the mother had two children, a son (Wally soul) and a daughter. The son often took care of his sister, but one time she wandered away, going into some nearby woods which apparently had been strictly off limits because of a hermit-type, deranged man who lived in a small hut in the woods.

While in the woods, away from the protection of her brother, the sister was attacked by this deranged man, brutally beating and raping her. The body was only found many weeks later. The mother blamed her son (the Wally soul) for this terrible murder since she felt it was his fault that his sister had wandered into the woods. This feeling of guilt within the Wally soul, and the deep anger within his mother in that lifetime, carried over into this lifetime.

Wally was an only child; his mother often told him about his very difficult birth, which left her unable to have more children. She totally blamed Wally for his divorce from his first wife, and constantly talked about "the family," which consisted of Wally's two daughters and his ex-wife. She considered his ex-wife as the daughter she never had, and she could do no wrong. The on-going conflicts between Wally and his mother were apparent to me early in our relationship, even though he always claimed to love her and certainly I believe he tried to love her. This is just one example of the many karmic relationships in Wally's most recent lifetime. What I finally understood before Wally's transition was the fact that this bizarre Soul Exchange he experienced before incarnating on Earth was an evolutionary leap that was quite traumatic for the soul. Accepting any spiritual beliefs, particularly my belief in extraterrestrials, walk-ins, reincarnation, etc., was to him frightening. His soul was saying, "Leave me alone with my scientific belief system, which makes sense to me. Don't try to push me into any higher evolutionary path. That is too frightening and I don't want to do that again!"

From following his progress on the other side after his transition, apparently his exposure to me and my belief system began to make sense to him when he began to do research in libraries on the other side. Finally in March of 1995, five months after his transition, Athor told me that Wally was assisting other souls who had recently left the Earth plane. She stated that this was under the supervision of more advanced souls.

It seems that he was assisting those who had lost their lives in the great Kobe, Japan earthquake, which would seem very appropriate considering his interest in geology. It would appear that he had made rapid progress on the other side, and I was very happy for him. Part of his Earth personality was helping other people, which was apparent from his experiences in hospital and skilled nursing facilities. Unlike many people, he much preferred being in a room with another person, because the nurses reported to me that he was always trying to help the other person in whatever capacity he was able to do under those circumstances.

I feel it was a great learning experience for me to have been with Wally for 25 years. He loved the Earth, and taught me a great deal about geology, keeping me grounded. Anyone into all of this "spacey" ET stuff really needs someone to keep them grounded to some extent here on Earth in order to survive the mundane tasks of living. That apparently was one of my jobs with Athor. She told me during our first session that she needed someone to keep her grounded during the time when she was doing readings. Being an Aquarian, I feel I am basically quite practical, despite all of my 'way out' beliefs!

Earlier in our marriage Wally was quite involved with the Association of Engineering Geologists (AEG,) often presenting workshops on the work he conducted for the California State Water Project, which included a system of dams and aqueducts. He encouraged me to begin presenting workshops on my work, something that I was reluctant to do, since I am basically a very introverted person. I gratefully give him credit for the path that my career took, even though he didn't share my beliefs. He was very opposed to my getting a Ph.D. in Psychology, mainly because it would take me away from home even more; but together we had a party to celebrate completion of my doctorate. I knew that he was always proud of what I had accomplished.

Chapter 7
Evelyn's Existences Off-Earth

Off Earth

Since the Athor reading requested in 1992 was for information on Off-Earth existences for both Wally and me, this chapter will first cover the Off-Earth reading for me and then other readings and regressions I have experienced. The Off-Earth readings for both Wally and me were conducted many weeks apart, with each reading being in two parts because Athor's energy did not last for much more than an hour at a time. I was amazed that each time when I asked about our Off-Earth relationship she would go into the same basic story, with some added details. If I ask her about a particular reading she would never consciously remember the details, but she could resume her reading of a particular soul's Akashic records as soon as she would go into a trance state.

You may notice that there seems to be a certain altered state of mind when one is reading about Off-Earth existences. I found this reading to be quite amazing! The following is the very lengthy reading which eventually involves both Wally and me. I considered eliminating part of this, but in the interest of perhaps helping people understand the grand evolutionary adventure of the soul I am including the material which made even me somewhat uncomfortable.

Athor: What we are seeing here, it's like a wall, but it's like a dimensional wall of energy, and it's over here. Then there's another wall over here, and the two come together (Athor is using hand motions.) It's not a fluidic motion the way humans are aware of. It's like a jarring and then integration, but it's not a fluidic kind of motion. From this motion of these two walls, there is created a space and in between the two so that for every movement when they come together there is a space. It's almost like a tunnel that is created, and it becomes longer and longer, then gradually wider and wider as these two walls separate more; the tunnel is wider and longer. You can see into it more, so we are going to go into it.

I haven't any idea what she is talking about and thinking, "Let's get on with it," but Athor was viewing all this as if it had some significance.

This is some type of existence which seems somewhat similar to the Earth. It's a beautiful nondimensional place. We see your traditional Pan-like creatures and more; this seems to be more of the true Devic realm. This is not on the Earth or near the Earth. This is probably the true home of the Devas before there were evolutionary changes, and certain of those souls and creatures chose to come into the Earth frequency. These are divine looking Beings who appear at this point. They are humanoid, but Beings of Light. They symbolically look like the priests and priestesses at the time when the Greek civilization was flourishing.

It would appear that since there was this dimensional doorway that this is also in another dimension. It was really when the void created this realm, this kingdom, the creation of the Devic Kingdom at the outset. All of these Beings existed together. They seemed to be at the same frequency level even though the forms they chose to take were different. They could all see each other, and they all existed in the same time and the same place. We pick out two in particular who didn't have any difference in form. They are all rather tall and lean, and seem to be clothed in gowns of Light, and the bodies were pretty much the same except in the species of the other Beings who are in different forms.

This was long before the inception of the Earth. This was a true representation of what the true Garden of Eden on Earth was to be, because all these Beings co-existed in peace and harmony. There was no competition and none of this type of activity.

Then there came a darkening. There is an overshadowing of the Light source to this plane. The Light seemed to penetrate everywhere. It never goes dark there. It was a muted light, but there was always light. Now we see here a darkening takes place, almost like a storm moving in – an energy storm. It's like a cosmic earthquake. It has a tremendous magnitude on this area. It's like a splitting. With this darkness that comes over it, there is this splitting again - this change. This is very strange. Half of this area we are reviewing, it's like an earthquake came and split this area in half, and you have one-half here, and one-half there of this particular scene we are viewing. And the one-half moves into a downward spiral and the other half moves into an upward spiral. And the downward spiral is moving toward a denser reality.

There's a tremendous lot of agitation and suffering that was not known before because there was no competition, no agitation, nothing but this very peaceful plane where nothing much went on. All of these Beings had co-existed in a very quiet, peaceful manner. Now with the onset of this energy, one-half is moving toward a greater density. All of the Beings going into a lower density are experiencing agitation which is something they never experienced before, and your soul went on the downward spiral. This was not just you; a whole group went through this experience. There's so much darkness and confusion.

We have one here who has plopped down on the planet, and this place is very foreign to you because there is darkness, not continuously, but there is a shifting between dark and light. The illumination on this planet and form which we see is also denser. It is humanoid only in that it has two legs and two arms and a tail-like appendage, and it is a humongous

66

change from this very ethereal plane. We are viewing this Being who is standing all alone in confusion and rage – in anger and with all these emotions that were not there before.

All of the Being's memory of its ethereal state is just gone. This is not the density of the Earth plane, but the Being was left without the memory of that prior place, perhaps for it to fully experience where it was, but it was very unhappy.

I was certainly not happy to hear about this bizarre existence, but putting it in perspective, this was just part of many evolutionary patterns.

This appeared to be a very barren looking place as opposed to the Garden of Eden type place we just saw. Everything is denser and bleaker looking. There are very few colors except for green and brown and occasionally gray. There is volcanic activity here.

There are other Beings, but this Being is alone. The others were spread out at this time. (Long pause, then Athor asks herself, "Why did you choose this place?") It was seen that the plane that these Beings existed on before was like a Garden of Eden, but it was seen that there would be no evolution from that place. It would just remain like that indefinitely. There was no potential for evolving. It was like the perfect place in many ways, but there could not be any growth. All of the Beings would never develop their consciousness beyond that level so this great cataclysmic event occurred and created these changes in these different energies, these polarities. The magnitude was simply beyond one Being's capacity.

This was something that happened on a dimensional level. It was one of those dimensional shifts that finally occurred which was very much needed, although it propelled half of these Beings. Those who spiraled down would have to work on their own to spiral up. So those Beings who were on the downward spiral chose to take this path because it was a big adventure.

Although the consciousness of those Beings was not sufficiently developed even in such a beautiful place, the consciousness per se, it was not an individualized identifiable choice as someone on Earth saying," I'll cross the street by this route rather than that route." It was nothing like that. It was on a soul level, and then it was perhaps more than just a single soul level, so all of these Beings went on the downward spiral for the purpose of then choosing to consciously work their way back up, so to speak.

It is so hard to describe, because then it was only in the soul state, and so in the interim right after losing that physical form, it returned back to its original soul state where the soul first manifested. Your soul returned to this plane in between cycles many times for nurturing - not with every physical cycle, but that is the soul's original identity when it first became a soul, when it first differentiated from the whole.

So this is the soul's identity as an individual soul, and your soul is from the Devic realm (In western metaphysics, the Devic energy is the spirit consciousness of mineral, plant, animal and more

68

subtle forms of fairies.) Each one has a very different soul identity. Once they become differentiated from the All, they each pick slightly different manifestations and experiences, etc. So your soul went back to the Devic Kingdom. Now it took the form of this little fairy like creature. It was unbounded in its freedom. It wanted to go back to where it had come from. But that plane no longer existed in the original form so it tried to go on the upward spiral to return to that form it had at the beginning, but it was able to get only so far. It wanted so desperately to get back, but it didn't quite get back.

So then it ended up in another dimensional frequency which was certainly much more evolved than the one it had dropped to but quite unlike what the upward half had gone to in the upward spiral. It visited a place that was similar to the place where it had first existed, but it was not that place. It was somewhere else. It was another creation elsewhere.

It was in this little flying form, and it came to this place where it had mountains, and they had a civilization. But it was not in the form the other Beings there were, and it was just kind of observing, wanting desperately to get back, knowing that there was something that was missing, and yet not understanding exactly what it was. There was this incredible pull, a longing, a yearning and this was as far as it could get at that point. The Beings would have stagnated on the original plane. They simply would not have evolved. This was seen as a deterrent. The whole creation has no place wherein that kind of situation can go on forever.

Change is the hallmark of all evolution and all existence. So this was an automatic thing that had to happen, but the Being remembered that it had something it wanted to get back to, but it didn't know exactly what it was, and since the change was part of the whole process, that's another reason it couldn't remember who it was. You could no longer stagnate spiritually. If you remembered where you came from, that's what would have happened. You would have created that for yourself, so that memory was blocked off for you.

That is another reason you have difficulty in this form regarding some of your consciousness, because there was that strong pull to return to that state, and that state was not moving, so no matter how nice and beautiful it was, until that cataclysmic event, it did not change.

Evelyn: What happened to the other Being you saw at the beginning of this reading?

Athor: It went on the upward spiral. The other Being was your twin soul and so that one went upward. This is very different from humans. There was not the yearning for other souls the way there are on other planes. There was not a strong sense of attachment. And so the other Being going on the upward spiral was not a devastating experience for you in any way because those heavy connections did not exist there.

Basically, your soul was pretty much individualized, but you spent a lot of time together there, but the bonds were much less than on other planes. The bonds were not restrictive, and spiritual energies would continue to be exchanged. So that memory was blocked there. But that little Being was aware there was something different. It was becoming merely the observer. It felt kind of a panic because it wanted to get back, but it could not.

So we see this little fairy-like Being, and it did not fit because the Beings were different. The other Beings could not see it because there was a difference in density as well. There was something on that plane that interested it, and it wanted to experience it. I'm not sure what it was, so it went into the form of one of the Beings being created there. It still retained its fairy form, but it was within this denser clothed form, and it was a unique experience because it was aware of its fairy-like form. It was aware of both forms at the same time. (This sounds akin to a Soul Braid in which two souls occupy the same body. Evelyn has had two cases of this type of "New Being" experiment.) So it was able to experience some of the things on that plane. It stored that information. It gave it another whole new dimension in consciousness and understanding.

One moment, please. Here again so many of these planes have this muted light. The Earth is really somewhat unique in that it has manifested a spiritual representation of the spiritual light. This other place was not dark, but it had muted, almost hazy light. There was a continuous source of light, but it never got lighter, and it never got darker. It was a little lighter than twilight.

This is the kind of general information that was given in many readings that seemed to have nothing to do with my particular soul.

Do you wish to go in slow progression or do you wish to ask questions?

Evelyn: Tell me something about the forms on that plane.

Athor: These forms had three eyes instead of two. Instead of ears, it had antennae apparatus to feel vibrations. It had three fingers like appendages to an arm, three leg-looking things.

Evelyn: Did these Beings go through life cycles like humans?

Athor: I don't know. They tended to prey on each other. They had a certain spot that was well guarded, because if this spot was attacked, then they could be preyed upon and that form could be exterminated because this was the center of the life force animating that form. There was no such thing as disease. There was simply a cycle of preying. This developed a species by learning where the others' Achilles heel were, because that was the only way they could be exterminated because they all had equal power. They all had equal strength, but they each had the one area that was like their Achilles heel. If that spot could be attacked in an unguarded moment, if that could be penetrated, then that physical form could be exterminated. In the process of extermination these Beings drew on the remaining life force of that Being and took it within itself and accumulated power. This eventually caused mutations in the species, and it brought about many changes. The species evolved this way. There really was no other way. It was quite an experience for you to occupy the body of one of the Beings. Your studies have taken you into many realms.

Evelyn: What happened after that cycle?

Athor: The Being seems to have taken on a similar form to the humanoid form in its original existence. We see a Madonna-like image with white robes. From this form comes forth a Being with wings. It is denser than the fairy form and much larger. It went into a plane that could self-propagate so it birthed itself in this form. It was flying over what appeared to be almost a watery-like substance. It is a shimmering substance. It's not a physical structure. How can I describe this? (Evelyn: Athor sees visual pictures, and then tries to interpret what she is seeing.)

It seems to have flown to a high spot in this place. It's almost like in Earth terms where the Greek and Tibetan monks used to live, similar type scenes. It sits there on this high spot, and it is in a pondering pose. There is still confusion, yet it is time to think, to try to get through the confusion of its origin. The soul always wanted to return to that original place. It did not have a conscious recollection, even in the Celestial plane prior to being individualized. It did not have a conscious recollection of the All That Is in its entirety. Perhaps that is because it simply could not. It wanted to go back to what it remembered, although it did not really remember. But there was the feeling or something to that Celestial realm, that place where there was none of these other things it is experiencing now.

So it was sitting there pondering and sort of thinking; then it flew over this place again where there was this shimmering look of water. At some point while it was flying over this shimmering place, it dove down and down into this shimmering place. It came to rest on somewhat firm ground. This appeared to be more physical than the other places. Here we see colors. Evidently, in this realm where it birthed itself, ah, this was the beginning of individualized awareness. It was the beginning of individualized spiritual awareness. That is what it was pondering, what was it going to do and where would it like to go?

It was at that point it became a matter of conscious choice. It was no longer a matter of it flew here, and this or that interested it. It made a deliberate choice. It went to this plane that had color and there was a sun and two moons. It was silvery, but it was very bright. The concept of greater or lesser does not exist in the soul. It is simply a construct of the mental faculties. To view these experiences of the soul's origin, and listening to them to employ that mental faculty and thus say, this was greater or lesser, has no bearing to the soul. (Evelyn: Again, Athor's insistence that we are all equal but simply all expressions of the All That Is evolving at our own rate.)

So then here we have this Being who appears to have wings, and is on this plane wherein there are two moons, and the ground substance is almost like a crystalline nature because it reflects the rays, and there is a tremendous light everywhere. It is a silvery light. This is the brightest light we have seen on any plane this Being has been upon up until this point. It is not a golden light like the Earth's light. There is much light, and because of these crystals there is much color.

A number of years after this I had a regression with Shirley Am-Ork, a friend I met at a conference in Southern California. When Shirley heard my talk at the conference about my work with Athor, she made it a point to get to know me, since she too felt strongly that she is a Soul Exchange. Subsequently she flew up to my office in northern California to do some regression work with me. She was a skilled hypnotherapist, and I felt very comfortable having a regression with her. I was amazed when I discovered that my home planet was Oxadoran, a planet in another galaxy outside the Milky Way. I only spelled it because I did not know how to pronounce it. I now assume that this is the planet, or perhaps plane is better terminology, that is being described by Athor. Many years later another client claimed that she too was from Oxadoran. I have never heard the name anywhere else, but I feel very definitely that this was where I first developed individualized consciousness. Later Athor confirmed that this planet was indeed Oxadoran.

The Being would appear to be the typical stereotype Angelic-looking Being. It does not appear to be ethereal, but more corporeal at this time we are viewing it. It has a tremendous amount of substance. The plane is also quite concrete. This is much denser, but you have all this light and crystals, so density does not refer to levels of evolution, per se, but it refers to the compaction of molecules, etc. So here we have a greater density as has heretofore been seen, except in that first instance of the reptilian Being, and that was totally different. There was no such lighting. And now here, the Being is somewhat isolated, and there appears to be some type of water similar to Earth but everything is crystalline, and everything is very beautiful. Here the Being is putting its hand over a particular facet of a crystal in the ground, and there is an exchange of energy with the warmth that is felt in the hand. There are a series of tones that begin to be emitted that begin from this interaction.

Apparently this is the beginning of my early relationship with Wally. It sounds fantastic, but Kevin Ryerson, the psychic who became very well-known through Shirley MacLaine, once told me that the way to get Wally tuned into metaphysics was to encourage his interest in crystals!

The Being is simply experimenting. It is very happy for the first time since leaving its original plane. It is similar in that there is no agitation, and no negativity. This is a new experience, a feeling it has never felt before. Now it is in a place where it is able to feel joy, and the joy came from discovery. This was the first time in this Being's awareness that it became conscious of the joy of discovery. This plane lent itself to much discovery — this interaction of certain crystals and energy fields. We see the Being both walks and flies.

Evelyn: Was it the decision of all of these souls from the Garden of Paradise (my term, for lack of better terminology) not to remember?

Athor: The souls upon that plane did not have a conscious awareness of an individualized state.

Evelyn: Did I have experiences on other star systems or planets?

Athor: You have been on Alpha Centauri. You have been on a galaxy which is not in your Milky Way, which is approximately nine to thirteen billion light years from this planet. It is to the left of the Milky Way galaxy, and as such, has not been named by the people of this planet Earth. It is most similar to this planet Earth. There are beings in this galactic system that are similar in structure to those on planet Earth. They exist in a multi-dimensional level; their physical bodies do not vibrate to the speed of sound, but vibrate to the speed of light, yet they have had similar histories in development to that of your planet Earth. It is upon this system that you made your choice and decisions to come to this plane to be of assistance to the evolutionary cycles here. (I think she is talking about Oxadoran, which was my home planet mentioned earlier, but at this point of the reading I did not ask that question.)

In addition, you had experience on Castor Pollex. You did not frequent many star systems, per se, since your interests led you elsewhere. However, the interest was not strong enough to bring you to any of these systems for any significant period of time. The energies were of such a fine level, and frequencies were such that it did not directly play into the forms you chose to inhabit or the places you chose to go to.

There also seems to be a connection to Andromeda. It would appear that there is a single star that the energies are beaming toward you for some reason. Whether this is in connection with the 11:11 activity it is not certain, but there is some star energy. It may be symbolic. I just see a very bright light but I don't see you there. It appears that this 11:11 beginning - not so much the event itself that day, but the opening and energy from that point on – that these energies will greatly assist you in allowing a block of energy to dissipate on a cellular level.

Evelyn: 11:11 was an event celebrated worldwide on January 11, 1992 to activate a pre-encoded cellular memory to open the doorway to a Higher Dimension. I coordinated this event for my area, with about 50 people from the California Sierra Nevada communities attending. The feedback indicated it was an amazing experience for everyone attending. As I am writing this I theorize that this was a step up in the evolutionary process of those attending all of these 11:11 events worldwide, the main location being the Great Pyramid in Egypt. Interestingly I am proof reading this the week of 11:11:11. Once again there will be worldwide events to raise the consciousness of humanity.

Your spirit is coming to a point when it is ready for it to remember. There is no longer a danger of the soul stagnating, but this is much more complex than the words would imply. Suffice it to say there is a star energy above you which is working through your energies helping to realign these energies.

Later, after writing this, I discovered another interesting reading from Athor:

Evelyn: Could you give me some information on the name that came to me just suddenly one night? It is

ARISTO, and I keep wondering what that name means to me.

Athor: It is that with which you are most familiar from the cycle of your expression, your embodiments, as it were, upon which you would term Venus. It would appear that you were there for approximately five Earth Cycles.

It is my understanding that indeed there is life on Venus, but not in physical type Earth bodies. The beings there function in Light bodies. Athor identified Venus as the home planet of one of my clients, who didn't seem at all surprised. She had always had a strong feeling about Venus. She was a school counselor who came for a reading prior to going to Morocco to work at the American School. She was a beautiful Being who certainly seemed to radiate Light.

Evelyn: Can we now proceed to my Earth lives?

Athor: You are one of the Fallen Angels. (Athor has ignored my question, but continued with this statement. What a shock to me!!) There was a plane on which the forces of the positive and negative became increasingly polarized to the point there was no total differentiation between the two, and absolutely no seeming connection between the two, although there is always a connection. It is all contained within the whole. It was another delusional aspect on that plane.

It seems there was an actual battle. This was a plane which was very close in proximity to the present Earth plane. This plane existed before the Earth plane existed. This plane was like your higher astral plane. This again is different from the Celestial.

So in the higher astral plane there was this big battle. The Beings utilized all kinds of forces and so forth until it was like an ethereal Atlantis. With all the forces used to bombard the energies, it created a rift. In the bottom of this plane, a big hole opened up so that no longer was this plane separated from the others. The disturbance was so great that it rent the ethers. In rending the ethers, this hole opened up, to which forces and energies came that started sucking and pulling on the Beings on this plane. As a consequence of which you, among many others, were pulled down through this magnetic and suctioning energy frequencies - it's like in a whirlwind almost – sucked in, and that was your entrance into the Earth's magnetic field.

You took some very slow steps to get to that density. If that had not occurred, you never would have reached that density, but because of what was going on in that plane, it was like an ethereal Atlantis. Atlantis was more physical than this. Perhaps some of the Atlanteans were just replaying what they had done on that plane. We (Evelyn: meaning the group soul, Athor) were not there, but we are seeing this now.

Evelyn: Which side was I on?

Athor: (laughs) You were of the Light. What I am seeing, you had already consciously come to the realization to go on the upward spiral, and as a result of the events upon that plane, and you just simply could not leave. There was a group consciousness which had developed, and all of this was intertwined so you could not just leave because all "Hell" was breaking loose, so you could not leave. You participated. It was almost like that was a test for you (Athor laughing again. I was simply overwhelmed and not very pleased with this information.)

If you had gotten out of there, it never would have happened, but because you felt you had to participate, that's when the chain reaction occurred. Even though you were in the Light and the polarities were differentiated, the mere fact that they became so differentiated was an illusion in and of itself. It is very difficult to describe, but it was an illusion. Most of the Beings there at that time, even the ones in the Light, could not see that. They were caught in that illusion of that polarity.

How interesting! Simply because you were in that consciousness of duality which was being manifested on that plane, that is why the plane opened up. The energies did what they did, and all of a sudden a bunch of you were going down to Earth. The ones who were in the dark, the so-called negative forces, many of them populated the lower astral of the Earth plane, because this was the higher astral plane where this occurred. So these dark ones populated the lower astral and were the beginning seed of what formed that dense ring around the Earth. In fact, they were some of the forerunners of some of the negativity on this planet. They formed that magnetic field which allowed for that potential.

I really did not understand this, but had found in the past if I tried to get a further explanation, Athor would go into

81

technicalities that I would understand even less, so I decided to move on in the reading. I certainly do not feel angelic although I have always been very attracted to angels and have a very large collection of various statuettes of angels. Perhaps the religious concept of the Fallen Angels is incorrect; rather these were simply souls that were of the Light that were sucked into the earth plane so interpreted as 'angels'. There is much literature to support the notion that the lower astral plane is populated by dark forces.

Evelyn: Okay, so I have been drawn into the magnetic force of the Earth. What happens now?

Athor: I see a flower, like a daisy, white with a yellow center, very tall, just swaying in the wind, coming from the Light. That was the least dense form you could occupy on this planet at that time. There is a subtle distinction here. It was you buying into the duality which happened on the higher astral that caused this to happen, for you to differentiate further from the Source. Since you were from the Light that was the lightest form you could take. You had very little to do with the Earth up until the time it became physical because you were in the higher astral plane. The higher astral is what the Christians talk about regarding the Fallen Angels.

This is where all that occurred. This was not in the highest so-called heavenly kingdom. To Earth Beings it may have appeared that way, but there are realms far beyond there. What went on in the higher astral is what eventually created the lower astral. Those Beings that were negatively polarized wanted to experience that concentrated energy that way.

This is all part of experience. To take and polarize the negative and the positive is just further differentiation and further experimentation. It is not the truth and reality of the whole. It is just a small aspect of it, and those Beings who wished to experience that, and thus polarize to that degree, got further and further away in consciousness from the Whole (the Source). Some who had similar frequencies went to other systems, but a big group stayed.

I really don't want to hear any more about the Fallen Angels since obviously this was an unpleasant memory in my consciousness, but Athor was fascinated by this so she had continued along that vein.

Evelyn: What happened next?
Athor: How interesting! I had always wondered about that. Wow! That is remarkable! We (Athor Group Soul) had not participated in that. Now I see a worm; this is kind of cute. Then I see a tree; the tree is changing and appears not to become a tree as a tree, but it was a conscious embodiment as a tree, like when you were a fairy. This is a similar type thing. You had the experience of what a tree felt like and what it experienced. (Evelyn: All of this is obviously more of the evolutionary process.)
Now we have a human type creature. It was a very long time ago. They are like the cavemen. They have a social structure government by "Might". We see here that one of these Beings sees a strange object in the sky, and you leave this group to go search because it looked like it went down to the ground. It looks to be

within walking distance. You are walking toward what you have seen. It takes about three hours of walking.

You find a strange vessel which has crashed to Earth. You are just amazed. You and your people have never seen anything like this. You touch the metal and it is hot. I see that the Being walked over to this craft which has sunk into the ground. It appears to be a circular craft, but almost half of it has sunk down into the Earth. It is not very large, but there is a strange noise coming forth from it, and there are just a few lights that are seen on it. The Being is most curious, and we see that the Being goes and tries to make physical contact with this craft by touching it, but it is very hot to the touch. At the same time there is a sensation. It is a very strange sensation because it's heat and icy coldness simultaneously which comes off the craft; the Being is just awed and amazed and a little frightened, but it is the strangest sensation it has ever experienced before, because to have a combination of both heat and icy coldness simultaneously was not possible on the Earth plane; that was mostly due to the fact that the craft's internal propulsion systems had malfunctioned so the balance of the energy produced a polarity of both extremes. (Evelyn: Maybe a physicist can figure this one out!)

They had lost control of the balancing mechanisms within the craft for their propulsion, so consequently the polarity was exhibited in the energy field of the craft because that was so typical of the Earth planet.

So we see the Being standing there. He's very puzzled, but he's not sure he wanted to touch it again because it was physically a very unpleasant sensation. He had no reference point to process that information, but he is most curious, and he is looking around and looking at it and trying to figure out what type of animal would make such a sound. He doesn't want to leave because this is like his prize find, but yet it is getting dark and he knows there are wild beasts out there so he had better get back to his people. He reluctantly goes back. He tells the other Beings of his find. He has no vocabulary to describe it so they decide to follow him at daybreak.

It is seen – oh my goodness! (Athor laughs) You started very early paying for your discoveries and your enlightenment, shall we say (much laughing. I have no idea what is so funny!) It is seen that the other Beings got in a fight because the other Beings decide they want this strange creature; so they fight you, and you are injured quite severely. They just leave you there. It is still daylight. They are trying to decide what they can do with this animal that doesn't move and doesn't breathe and they can't eat it. They have figured out that it is very hard, but they want to do something with it. You are just lying there. Somebody has knocked you unconscious because they had decided it was theirs and not yours. This is really humorous to watch! It is seen that this small craft is perhaps in its dying throes as the tones are increasing.

Evelyn: Are there any Beings in the craft?

Athor: We are not seeing that. But the tones become so loud that you wake up, and it is very piercing to the eardrums, so you try to move away from the craft. But in the dying throes, this craft is giving off a tremendous magnetic field that escaped because of the problems it had, that is, why it crashed - the lack of the harmonizing, stabilizing factor within the ship's propulsion system. So this magnetic field just pulses out from the craft around it, and it hits you; it is almost like a sensation of being in a tremendous wind. There is no wind, only this high frequency pulsation. You are kind of trapped in the field for a little while.

Then the final mechanism shuts down within the craft, the magnetic field is propelled outward. It's pushed outward, and you are in it; you are thrown up against the boulders by this force. Then there is no more sound, and the craft lies dead and still. When you have regained your composure, you walk over there to touch it again. This time there was no sensation. The craft was dead so that was a curious thing to you. There was no comprehension, of course, but it sparked a whole lot of curiosity to the brain centers. How did this happen, etc.? There were only questions and curiosity because there was no reference.

The other Beings thought they had killed you, so they were surprised when you returned to the group. Those Beings had a rudimentary level of consciousness similar to your present ape-like creatures, in that their socialization was such they would have big fights. They did not have sufficient consciousness to feel guilt, so did not give thought to what had occurred, as animals have also not developed that sense except the domesticated ones; the wild animals generally do not. This was like when monkeys and apes get together they would have a fight then they make up. It's no big deal, so they were not concerned when you showed up even though they thought you were dead.

There was this communication again as to what had happened to the craft, so they all went out again the next day. They all touched it, but the magic was gone. They had wanted to possess it because it had magic; it had a sound, a strange noise and lights. When it was dead, they did not want it. So the craft just remained there. They didn't do anything with it. There were no visible doors to the craft because these had been sealed by the mechanism before it had crashed. Actually, this craft had the capacity to change and transmute from one level to another so they can appear to manifest in a physical realm. It was because of the malfunction of the propulsion system that caused it to crash and become materialized. That is the primary nature of any of the crashes that occur. Before any of these crafts crash, they have been in the nonphysical form of energy expansion. There's a certain system of contraction and expansion of energy systems that has to occur in order for an object to materialize. This is akin to the manifestation process upon this plane as well, but that is another subject.

This was obviously my first encounter with a space craft here on Earth. I have always accepted the fact that there are space crafts and extraterrestrials. Perhaps this encounter registered at a deep subconscious level.

Evelyn: Let's move forward to any particular lives that have impacted the present time.

Athor: At this time instead of going into individual lives, the one thread that has continued throughout Earth lives is that sense of adventure, that sense of curiosity, that exploratory open minded faculty. Though it has not exhibited this in each and every cycle, it has been one of the main threads which has kept this soul quite firmly linked to its source. There was one link of light or one series of links of lights, which did not die out, you might say. So no matter what the life cycles were, it was not sufficiently dimmed. This is a somewhat unusual quality because it has carried over this link for such a long period of time.

Evelyn: About how many lives have I lived on Earth?

Athor: At this time we get approximately 220-225.

Evelyn: Why is it so difficult for me to tune into my own past lives?

Athor: I am looking at your energy system. It is seen there is a seal on the third eye. The seal has been placed there for your own protection. It will not be removed until such time when, by opening it, you will not lose that protection. When the Earth frequencies reach a certain point, that seal will be unlocked. We do not see that this has been placed there through your own making.

Evelyn: Did I have any experience with any Beings I presently know on Earth prior to coming to Earth?

Athor: It seems that the one who is presently your husband, (Wally) is one such Being. This is very difficult to describe. The Beings that we are viewing here appear to be similar to your gnome-like creatures, but different because the substance is in continual motion with these forms. The representation would be like ectoplasm; it isn't a mist type thing, but it has some form and some density and some substance to it. It is more like a mixture between a gaseous and liquid substance wherein they are somewhat fluidic, but it is not fluidic as water. It is almost like viewing an amoeba, and you watch the expanding and pulsating and it changes shape, etc.

We are trying to comprehend this realm. It is very unusual, very different, almost like an amoeba, but the amoeba is filled with the essence of life, and it is filled with the potential of life within it. Upon this plane these Beings are a similar representation of the beginning of life of their particular evolutionary strain. As such, they had a similar rudimentary consciousness which is not as evolved. The frequency is not as slow as the Earth amoeba; however, it is not one of great insight and self-knowledge. It is almost like an experiment.

We see that you are not one of these Beings, but you were having something to do with them upon that plane. I'm sorry, but I have to laugh, because it was almost like the Beings where you came from. These were like your pets, and you and others had some hand in helping them evolve in either creating them, or helping them expand; something to that effect. Whether they were actually created by you and others, I don't believe was quite the case, but there was this connection. They were like pets, so your Beings by interacting with these Beings helped them evolve.

This would suggest that when our beloved pets are around us they are reaching the stage of their evolution when they may incarnate as a human baby in the future.

Evelyn: Where was this system?
Athor: This is a system far removed from yours. It is not within this galactic system. Your astronomers do not have a complete picture of the universe as a whole. What to them is known is just a small speck. It is very, very far away from this galactic system, in another galaxy.
Evelyn: The latter part of this is some repetition and elaboration of the reading discussing my early Off-Earth interaction with Wally.

This ended the reading, which had been conducted in two sessions more than three weeks apart. The second session had begun with my instructing Athor in the induction to pick up my soul records when I finally incarnated on Earth. While there is much I do not understand, I am including the entire reading with the hope that the readers will get a good taste of the very long evolutionary process of the soul. Even though this reading is quite long, it, of course, only touches on a small portion of my soul history.

Chapter 8

Evelyn's Past Lives Through Regression

Bandon Sunset

An important part of the training to be a past life therapist is to have the experience of going into a past life yourself. I am basically a very poor hypnotic subject, since I do not get visual pictures when my eyes are closed. My clients who were able to get visual pictures had the greatest success in feeling as if they were actually seeing a past life. Those who are kinesthetic also were able to feel what was happening to them. Then there are those like myself who simply use their so-called imagination.

The first regression I experienced was conducted by a man who taught electronics at American River College in Sacramento and did past life regressions as a hobby. After a lengthy induction I felt that I was being hung as a witch for the work that I was doing with herbs. There were more details which some thirty plus years later I do not recall, but when I came out of that trance state Larry told me he could see red welts around my neck from rope burns.

Several nights later I was sitting at the dinner table after a very long, tiring day at my job as a counselor in the school system, when I suddenly started screaming. That totally freaked my husband out. I tried to tell him I was all right, to just let me alone. During this episode I KNEW I was being hung, and it was totally unjust. I started crying, and went into the bathroom to wash my face. When I looked in the mirror I saw the image of a very old woman, totally unlike my normal face. After a good night's sleep, I was fine the next day, but the result of all this was a huge difference in my ability to do public speaking.

Part of my job as a high school counselor was to talk to parent groups. I would get what I later recognized as panic attacks prior to doing these talks; my heart would beat very fast, and I always felt as if my neck was very hot and red. However, after this regression, this no longer happened. I am still not totally comfortable talking to large groups, but after From Sirius to Earth was published I was able to give many presentations with hundreds of people in the audience. I theorize that the screaming episode released the energy from my cells which had resulted from being hung as a witch.

Apparently in that past life I made the mistake of talking about my beliefs and the seed thought was planted in my subconscious mind that talking about your beliefs results in being hung. I was still in the early stages of believing in reincarnation, extraterrestrials, etc., all of these "way out" beliefs that were definitely not main stream thinking at the time. While I certainly did not talk about these things when talking to groups of people, apparently just the thought of public speaking was equated with being hung; in fact, just talking to anyone did not come easily for me; I was an extremely shy child. I have a friend who tells the story of my visiting her when I was about five years old, and she pushed me down some steps because I wouldn't talk! When I was a therapist some of my clients were able to release similar energies that resulted in quickly releasing present day problems.

During the time I was on the Board of Directors for The Association of Past Life Research and Therapies (now the International Association for Research and Therapies (IARRT,) we had board meetings several times a year. Dr. Hazel Denning was the President for many years, and then became Executive Director of the organization. After one of the meetings at the old Astara Campus in Upland, California, I asked Hazel if she would do a regression for me. I was amazed as I began telling a story of being a caveman and killing my wife with a club. I hid her body, but the clan discovered the body and banished me from the clan. It was almost impossible to live alone in those early days. I was crushed beneath the feet of a mammoth, having failed to kill it with my spear. When asked why I had killed my wife, I replied, "Because she could not have children."

I thought I had come to terms many years earlier over the issue of my inability to have children in this lifetime, but this seemed to be the karmic reason for this. As mentioned earlier, I had been told by several psychics that having children was simply not my purpose in this lifetime. I believe, considering my low energy level, I could not have had a career and done an adequate job of parenting. However, there was some subconscious thought that I must have done something wrong to deserve this "karma". Wally and I were having serious problems at that point, so my first thought afterward was, "Was Wally the wife I killed?"

Subsequent hypnotic sessions, plus Athor's input, was "no," and that was a relief. My other thought was, "Could my ongoing back problems be the root cause of having been crushed by the mammoth?" Perhaps, but going through the regression did nothing to relieve my back problems.

While still in a trance state with Hazel Denning, I recalled another lifetime when I had stabbed a man in a bar fight. As a punishment I was put in a cage. People ridiculed me and threw things at me. I recall (I think) that I finally went mad. This seemed to be during Medieval Europe.

I can't imagine simply making up such unpleasant things about myself. In trying to analyze this, if indeed these lifetimes were true, it would seem that people can make a turning point toward the better in their lives. Apparently as one of the "Fallen Angels," I began the whole Earth experience, evolving from a primitive man through being a murderer; and then began the upward spiral to become a so-called witch, then progressing to my most recent past life as the son of a wealthy tailor in London, England.

Now that is one scenario; on the other hand I felt a strong familiarity with places in Egypt, Greece, and Peru during my travels to those countries. It would seem that my past lives on Earth were not a continuous upward spiral, since according to Athor readings I discovered that each soul seems to have a predestined pattern. As with my evolvement before coming to Earth, my soul was open to many adventures and experiences. We are all expressions of the Source, with many different paths. My mother was greatly disturbed at times due to my adventuresome nature!

Another possible explanation of past life memories may be that we are tapping into the past lives of other aspects of our soul. In my work with a number of clients, I found the time frame of some of their past life memories overlapped. For instance, in one past life the person was born in 1840 and died in 1890; in another life period the birth occurred in 1862 and death in 1880. Actually not many clients were able to give exact dates, but when this happened and they questioned me after the regressions, my only explanation was perhaps they were tapping into the life of another aspect of their soul. In a hypnotic state one is often able to tap into the all-knowing universal mind. At some level we are all related. A few times they were tapping into the past life of an attached entity, but that was extremely rare. I really did not enjoy dealing with attached entities, but when an earthbound spirit attaches to a person it can cause havoc in their lives; therefore, I feel that a therapist should know how to handle cases of this nature; however, that is an involved subject not relevant to this book. Obviously there is much about past life regressions I still do not understand, but I am totally convinced that it is an extremely effective method of therapy.

I had several regressions with another friend I met at one of the Past Life Therapists Conference. The most interesting part of these regressions was remembering the name of my home planet, Oxadoran, which was mentioned earlier. I could not pronounce it, so spelled it out slowly letter by letter. The home planet is where the soul first has an individualized consciousness. Earth was Wally's home planet.

He was fascinated by geology and felt very much as if he belonged on Earth. On the other hand, I have never really felt at home here, even though I have had many past lives on Earth. Apparently my Off-Earth lives left a much stronger impression upon my subconscious than my Earth lives.

In my metaphysical work, many of my clients felt as I do. They sensed no strong connection with the Earth. One particularly psychic client, who had been paralyzed and in a wheelchair since early childhood, amazed me when she informed me that she too was from Oxadoran. She lived with her mate, who was a brilliant retired college professor. She recalled Off-Earth past lives between the two of them in which he was a scientist and performed all kinds of bizarre experiments on her. I often thought that taking care of her as he did for many years before her death was a huge burden for him. On the other hand, he seemed totally devoted to her; she and I felt that he was probably balancing out karma in a big way.

Since, according to Athor, Wally and I had a pattern of many lives together, both negative and positive; we were together again to balance out our karma. We had some wonderful years together during the early part of our marriage, but during the latter days of our relationship I often considered getting a divorce. Wally, being a Cancer and with a birth path of 6 according to numerology (family, nurturing, caregiver, etc.) refused to even consider this. He clung to me tenaciously, and made it clear that we would have a big court battle if I pursued this path. I was in the midst of obtaining my doctoral degree and did not feel I was up to a big fight. By being away from home a great deal attending conferences, giving workshops, etc., I was able to stay in the marriage for which, in retrospect, I am very grateful. Wally was a good man, and I really loved him dearly despite our problems. Although he was not happy about my being away from home so much, he encouraged me to give workshops and write my two books, *You Are Wonderful* (a manual on self-esteem based on my Ph.D. dissertation research) and *From Sirius to Earth*. He also supported the idea of adding on a very large addition to our home, an office which allowed me to have total privacy for my therapy practice, and an adjacent room large enough to have group meetings.

Wally was in and out of hospitals and rehabilitation nursing facilities many times before his transition in 1994. Unfortunately, his leukemia was not diagnosed soon enough to receive any medical help, with the exception of frequent blood transfusions. It was his desire to die at home. He lived long enough for visits from his two daughters and former wife, and then lapsed into a coma for a week before passing over. His last words were, "I don't want to die and leave you." I am extremely grateful for my 25 year marriage to Wally; he was really a very beautiful, though young, soul.

Chapter 9

Ed, My Air Force Colonel Husband

Colonel Cook

My husband, Wally, died of leukemia in 1994. In 1999, I met Colonel Edwin Cook at a widowed person's organization dinner in Roseville, California. There were mostly widows attending, and they swarmed around Ed, he being a new member and widowers were scarce in the group. While waiting to be seated at the dinner table, Ed overheard me talking and noted my Southern accent. He made it a point to sit near me at dinner because he had a deep love of the South, having been stationed at numerous bases throughout the South during his pilot training. I had grown up in Georgia. Ed attended cadet pilot training at Cochran Field, which was near my childhood home, during World War II. At the time I was only 11, while Ed was 18, so I never encountered him during his stay at Cochran, which is now the airport for Macon, Georgia. Our family would often go over to nearby Harris Field to watch the pilots from Cochran practice touch and go landings.

During the course of the evening I mentioned to a lady sitting next to me that I had a new barbecue that I couldn't get to work. I, of course, wanted Ed to overhear this conversation and offer to help me with the barbecue. For years I wouldn't admit to this ploy but indeed Ed offered to follow me home to see what he could do to get the barbecue started. Later I wondered why I so readily agreed to this. He was unsuccessful in starting the barbecue and advised me to return it to the store since it obviously was defective. However, after that he stayed and visited for several hours. There must have been some kind of soul recognition from the beginning. After that evening, Ed came on really strong, which freaked me out since I was not ready to get into an in-depth relationship with another man. He invited me to his ranch for several elegant meals, and within three weeks asked me to marry him. Since I was soon going back to my home town in Georgia for my 50th high school reunion, I thought it would be nice to have a companion for the trip so I agreed, with the understanding that it would be a long engagement. It seemed to be more respectable if we were engaged.

Chapter 9 | Ed, My Air Force Colonel Husband

Ed and I did a great deal of traveling during our early days together - Spain, Tunisia, Sweden, England, Scotland, Alaska, Mexico, Canada and Venezuela. In 2000 during a cruise to various islands in the Caribbean, Ed decided that it would be very romantic to get married on board our Greek registered ship. I finally went along with this because it would not be legal. We had a beautiful wedding with the ship captain officiating, an orchestra, champagne, delicious cake, many lovely flowers and a number of the ship's passengers attending. It would not be until exactly one year later that we were finally legally married at an Air Force Chapel at Travis Air Force Base in California. It was December 2001 not very long after 9/11, and there was very tight security at Travis. With only a best man and maid of honor attending, this was quite a contrast from our lovely shipboard wedding!

There were a number of reasons for my indecision to marry Ed. He told me the second time I saw him that he had prostate cancer. It seemed to be well controlled with hormone therapy, but having lived through many years with my husband Wally, who was 11 years older than I, and disabled for a number of years prior to being diagnosed with leukemia, I was very hesitant to go through anything like that again. Being a caregiver is an extremely difficult job. I understood that with Wally I was being given a soul lesson to give me patience, not one of my innate talents. I thought I had learned that lesson reasonably well; I didn't think I needed a graduate degree! Ed had lost his wife to breast cancer. She was a Lt. Colonel, serving as a nurse in charge of medical evacuation flights out of Vietnam. He too was reluctant to get into a long term caregiver role as he was for many years with Lindy. One of his comments to me was "When you are my age, you don't have much time to waste". Plus he had made it clear that he was very much in love with me. Not long after we had met, he was at my house and we were discussing the marriage issue. I again told him I did not want to get married. He said something to the effect, "Then I guess this is goodbye" and he left the house with tears in his eyes. After hearing nothing from Ed for almost a week, I relented, calling him and saying that maybe we could eventually be married.

His remark regarding limited time turned out to be unfortunately quite true. There was another reason I was a reluctant bride. From the very beginning of my relationship with Ed I was appalled at how much he talked. When I finally brought this to his attention he stated that he had said all of the important things that he wanted to say so the talking would slow down. This, of course, was really impossible for Ed because he was a "people person", a true ambassador to the world, as many of his foreign friends stated when they heard of Ed's death. He loved giving speeches, could tell really funny jokes, and had an extremely extroverted personality, a total opposite of me! However, he believed in UFOs and thought the concept of past lives was very interesting.

Ed was a 50 year Mason, a Shriner, and member of Scottish Rite, with a deep spiritual belief in God. These were good qualities, and all of the women at the widow's group in Sacramento (a much larger group than Roseville) were fawning over Ed when we attended a big Halloween party. I concluded that lots of older women wanted Ed so maybe I should be more accepting of all of his talking. Certainly he was never dull!

After the death of my husband Wally, prior to meeting Ed, I had met three other interesting men, but because of my conflicts with Wally regarding my belief system, I asked Athor to do a reading to give me an understanding of their soul pattern and my soul connection (if any) with them. In each case there was indeed a soul connection, but they were not suitable partners for me in this lifetime. Although I was opposed to getting married again, I would have enjoyed the companionship of an interesting man. With Ed, since he wanted to get serious so quickly, I invited Athor to have dinner at my home with Ed and me so she could meet him in person. It was instant approval; she could see "Light" in Ed's eyes, and commented that I had finally met someone who was compatible with my soul. Her stamp of approval gave me more confidence to proceed with a more serious relationship.

In retrospect, I was more attracted to other men on a physical level because there was more of an emotional involvement. Because Ed's malignant prostate had been removed through surgery, our sexual attempts were more funny than ecstatic! Ed made me laugh and we were very affectionate; I probably was not "in love" but I loved him at a deep level. I was honored to have been his wife for almost ten years prior to his transition.

Being with Ed certainly convinced me of the necessity of having a strong military force, until the Earth evolves to the point this will no longer be necessary.

Very soon after meeting Ed, I told him that I wanted him to read my book, *From Sirius to Earth,* before we even thought about being in a serious relationship. I gave him a copy, and he assured me that he had read it. His only comment was that he "had no problem with it." The main point that he apparently gleaned from the book was the concept that there are many Councils who help God. I must say I never even thought of it that way, but of course that is so true. Ed had given up on organized religion many years before we met. He was the Superintendent of the Sunday School in a very large church in Sacramento, but became quite disillusioned over many things happening in the church. That was the end of his attending church.

Ed's goal in moving to Oregon from California was to have another boat to go fishing. We both love seafood, particularly crab, which can be caught from the dock in Bandon. He had sold his six acre ranch outside of Sacramento CA in 2007, getting a very good price for it. On the property there was a huge barn Ed had built to house all his "stuff" and his toys. Two large dumpsters were filled, but there was still much left in the barn so before we had found a house to buy in Bandon, he had another barn built to house all the remaining "stuff".

Due to the change in the economy I had great difficulty selling my home so I could not make the final move to Oregon until July 2008. Some very good friends of Ed's were staying in their motor home at an RV park in Bandon that summer. We spent many days playing bridge, one of Ed's passions. It was a very enjoyable summer, up until August 8 when Ed had another intestinal block which required surgery. He developed an infection in the hospital; therefore, spending most of his remaining life in and out of various hospitals until he passed away on May 7, 2009. One infection after another had put his prostate cancer into high gear. He had no quality of life toward the end, so as Athor has said, "His soul was ready to leave quite a while before his actual transition".

Ed was buried in Arlington National Cemetery, with full military honors. I was totally awe struck when leaving the nearby chapel at Fort Myers. There was a full Air Force Band, caisson with white horses, and the Honor Guard that accompanied us to his gravesite. Ed's son had the presence of mind to ask for the bullets that were fired in the 21 gun salute.

I was in such a daze the entire day that I never would have thought of that. Ed's best friend, Dr. Brice Wilson, who gave the eulogy, later put the bullets on plaques which he gave to various people. Arlington Cemetery is a beautiful place; I had seen their ceremonies on television and in movies but certainly never dreamed my husband would actually be buried there. It was a surreal experience and I was grateful that I was able to make the trip to Washington.

Three weeks prior to the Arlington service I was in the hospital in Eugene having three stents placed in my arteries. The doctors recommended open heart surgery, but I told them there was no way I was going to miss my husband's burial at Arlington.

After returning home, I foolishly decided to take advantage of a time share that I had reserved in the Mt. Hood area. Ed and I had already canceled three trips due to his physical problems, and I was determined to go on this trip, even though I would be going alone. It was a very rainy day in early November when I started on this trek. Going through Portland was a nightmare; I became thoroughly lost, having turned off from the freeway too soon for my destination. I finally stopped at a Burger King and an elderly couple who were having lunch there took pity on me and suggested I follow them all the way to my final turnoff; they lived in the direction of Mt. Hood. I failed to get their names but truly felt they were my angels that day, as they made sure I was always behind them on crowded freeways and streets.

By the time I reached my destination at the resort in Welches, it was snowing. After buying some food supplies at a local grocery store I hunkered down and did almost nothing the entire week except transcribe an autobiography Ed had written toward the end of his life. I learned to use Ed's laptop as I tried to decipher his small hand written saga. Unfortunately he was unable to get past his years in the service during World War II. The following are a few of the more interesting excerpts: I am including these because they seem to be of historical interest – a time in the early history of San Francisco.

When I was two years old in 1927, Charles Lindberg, having flown across the Atlantic, paraded down Market Street in San Francisco where I was born. My mother said she had taken me to the parade where she took my hand and touched Lindbergh with it. I believe that from that time my destiny was to be in aviation.

My earliest memories were of the great depression. I remember sitting at our window looking down Grove Street to Market Street at all the autos going by. Then there were few cars going by when the depression hit.

There was a "soup" line down the street. I remember a lady wearing a beautiful fur coat standing in line to get something to eat. At one point, my father and I were walking down Market Street and I asked him who those men were selling pencils. His answer was they were veterans.

My father's employer, Western Meat Company, allowed the employees to take meat home for their families. I do not remember a lack of food, but I do know that times were lean. Our economic situation improved when Dad received an increase in salary from $25 a week to $27.50.

Through most of those years we kids had cardboard in our shoes to cover the holes, and patched pants. Those memories have certainly had an influence in my life. Even today, money in the bank does not mean as much as a full larder.

Ed bought large quantities of food if he found a "good buy." After his death I spent many hours throwing away, or giving to the food shelter great quantities of outdated canned goods, spices, etc. Ed had a barn full of things he "might use someday" that he moved up to Oregon. I had to dispose of all these things after Ed died. I truly believe that the great depression left a deep impression in his subconscious mind. This seems to be the case with many of the people who went through that very difficult period of our history.

Our house was in the Golden Gate Heights, and was really like being in the country at that time. I really had little interest in school and much preferred hunting cottontails with my slingshot, climbing the trees and cliffs, or lying on the grass or on the bough of a tree and watching the clouds roll by.

I believe it was once a year that the Fleet would visit San Francisco. Of course the event was well publicized in advance. Mother would pack me a lunch and I would climb to a high point on the hills above our home on Noriega Street and watch as the Fleet came in the Golden Gate. Later when they began to build the Golden Gate and Bay Bridges, from my perch high up on the sand dunes I could review the progress of spanning the cables across San Francisco Bay. I miss the nostalgia of riding the ferry boats back and forth across the Bay, and I certainly do not appreciate all the traffic congestion the bridges have brought.

Today it is hard to believe, but as a child we kids could go about the city on the street cars alone and never be molested. We had those big Irish policemen with their clubs, and no one would think of hurting a child when these guys were around. From time to time we kids would take the streetcar to Chinatown and buy bait and then another streetcar to Fisherman's Wharf to fish. We were only eight to nine years old, but no one ever had a problem.

When I was nine years old my father accepted an offer to go to Sacramento and open the fresh meat business for the Purina Sausage Company. I turned over a new leaf and became a good student, receiving "satisfactory" on all my report cards the rest of elementary school.

In high school Ed was told by his guidance counselor that he was really not college material, which seems incredible to me. Ed completed college after he joined the service, plus finishing the coursework at the Air Force War College, which was mandatory for everyone who aspired to be a colonel. I have read a number of the papers he wrote which I felt were excellent. While we were married I always asked him to proofread anything I wrote, and he often made corrections which I agreed improved my writing. I guess the moral of this is, you cannot predict one's future by what they do in high school. Ed also reminded me that he was working a full time job through high school and college. I would certainly have flunked out of Agnes Scott College had I been working as he did.

Both Ed's mother and father were extremely good looking people, but their relationship was apparently stormy from the beginning. There was every indication that they truly loved each other, but did not get along very well. Ed's father was raised by his grandparents, who were extremely strict. His father told stories of being beaten when he was a child; that was all he apparently knew about being a parent. Ed told me about his father having a bull whip at the dinner table, and if he got out of line he would be beaten either with the whip or his father's belt. Ed always resented his father, but in his autobiography he wrote that he thought his father did the best he could, and seemingly had forgiven his father.

When Ed had an Athor reading and asked about his father, Athor gave a long narrative about how both Ed and his father had been leaders of a group of people coming out west in the 1800's. They had a disagreement over which route to take. Ed went north with some of the group, and his father continued on over the mountains, were snowed in, and many of the people died. It sounded like a story akin to the Donner party in which most of the people died, although she did not identify the group of people. Apparently this disagreement between the leaders was quite antagonistic, and Ed blamed his father when he heard about so many of his friends dying. His father no doubt felt extremely guilty over making such a poor decision. As was the usual pattern, these two were together in other lifetimes and were together again in this lifetime to balance their karma. I'm sure Ed has no desire to be with his father again, but with his belief in reincarnation, he tried very hard to get along with his father, although from what I observed that was rather one sided.

As a therapist, it was my hope that when I did a past life regression at his request, Ed would go back to a lifetime with his father. It seemed to me that there was still a great need for him to forgive his father for his abusive treatment. However, what he "remembered" was being with Sir Francis Drake and Napoleon, both of whom fascinated him in this lifetime. Although we never had a reading from Religious Research because Dr. Franklin Loehr had passed over by the time Ed and I were together, I would guess that Ed was a well-along soul. He was a natural leader, and never met a stranger. As I told the group who attended the luncheon at Fort Myers Officer's Club after Ed's burial at Arlington, I felt it was a real privilege to have been his wife.

Because we were so very different I wanted to know more about our soul connection. According to Athor, we were good friends in a life in Egypt, husband and wife on an island in the south Pacific, and relatives in Paraguay. We both had some difficulty connecting with the life in the south Pacific; Ed was an obese native king, such as it was on a small island, surrounded by adoring young girls. He imbibed too much of some of the native plants, which had the effect of putting him in a kind of stupor, and that resulted in his being a very poor king. As his wife, I knew that the island was going to be invaded by natives from a neighboring island and urged my husband to prepare our village, but he did nothing, and most of our village was wiped out when they attacked us. Perhaps he learned that this was not the way to be a leader! This scenario was certainly nothing like the Ed in our relationship, although I often felt impatient with Ed, which probably reflected that lifetime.

The lifetime that was very meaningful to us both was the one in Paraguay. We were both members of a politically prominent family. I had been captured and held for ransom. Ed rescued me, but in the process was captured and hung.

110

Another lifetime which really resonated with Ed was his life as a Viking. His group of Vikings had landed at a small settlement; they were in the process of sacking the village and raping most of the women. I was living in one house with a small child. Ed took pity on me and saw to it that I was not harmed. He always had a fascination with the Vikings. Twice Ed had rescued me in past lives. I have never felt the need to be rescued in this lifetime, but I feel that my taking care of Ed through all of his physical problems was my payback for his saving my life in prior lives. This was not negative karma but a balancing of our mutual services to each other. Athor stated that we had never had major conflicts in any past life, nor were we romantically involved before, but our souls were happy to find each other again. I was devastated when he died although I knew he would be better off, as he was released from the problems with his physical body.

111

Chapter 10

Ed's Off-Earth Existences

Evelyn at Ed's burial at Arlington, Oct. 2009.

About a year after I had met Ed, I asked Athor to do a Soul Source reading for him.

Athor: We have here a scene of something that looks like the Fourth of July fireworks. There are many multicolored lights. Then there is an explosion. All of these lights seem to either go somewhere or dissipate. The energy is then going into this center of a golden ball. It is sort of like time travel. There appears to be tremendous pressure like G forces going through this ball. (Pauses)

We have here a scene that appears to have tropical, lush looking vegetation. It is not physical. There are some types of birds but different types of plant life than what we commonly have here today. There are some plants with very large leaves that take in nutrients by opening cells with this huge pod. Each leaf is like a pod, and it has something like gills in it. It takes in nutrients in some type of respiratory process.

These plants go far down into the surface of this area, and they have a vast root-like structure. This is unusual because these roots go down and form some type of life supporting mechanism for a life form under the surface of this area. They would be similar to today's trees, in a sense, and there are tiny creatures under there that have more than a rudimentary form of intelligence. They are much larger than insects, perhaps a bit bigger than the size of a rat. Sometimes they can walk on two feet, but generally they scurry about on all four. They are sort of like a rodent type of thing, but they don't look quite like a rodent. So these plant life forms are providing some type of both protection and nourishment for these little creatures under the ground.

Now we are seeing several life forms. These are a higher form than the one just described, and there appears to be a consciousness with this type of life form. We don't see that there was just one form that the consciousness of the Ed soul went into. It is more like it was a whole group. Basically, they just primarily existed. There was a form of intelligence, but not like anything that is known in the human realm. This was a much different life form. There appears to be a strong connection with this soul with vegetation forms - the plant kingdom, that type of sensitivity which has gone through many, many periods of evolution while the Being was on Earth, and it has changed. It has become much more structured and much more physical, so that the Being itself embodies a great deal of this energy. It is difficult to describe.

This certainly makes no sense to me, except it apparently is another type of evolutionary journey before developing an individualized consciousness.

Evelyn: (trying to understand this) This consciousness of the Ed Being was in the plant life form or this group of small creatures?
Athor: No, it is in the more advanced plant life form that was not stationary. It appears that there was a group consciousness. Now we again have this time travel effect. We have here a star system wherein there appears to be no sun as we know it here on Earth. This appears to be primarily twilight, although there are two moons, two sources of Light which are not suns, but is never fully dark. The system takes twenty-four days for the phase to change in the lighting.

These beings are very tall. They are very thin and have a smooth, almost slippery, type of skin. They have three long claw-like fingers, and one almost like a thumb. They have large ears that are pointed on both top and bottom. The ears are more like in a canine. They are able to move the ears like a radar type device. There is no hair on the body, the head, or anywhere else. The faces have two very large sunken-in eyes. The orbits are perfectly round and totally dark. There does not appear to be a pupil as we know it, but a shutter mechanism that allows for the changes in the lighting so that the beings adjust to this lighting. They would be completely photosensitive since they are not geared to sunlight at all. There do not appear to be noses, but rather slits, indentations and a very, very small mouth. It is almost like a straight line. It appears that this is the Zeta Reticula system. They have just gotten to the point where they have learned about space travel. They have finally achieved the level where they can travel to other systems.

There is a bunch of talking, making plans for an expedition somewhere. There is some disagreement because some of them believe they should do this or that, and so forth. There is one Being that is not part of all of this disagreement; he basically is taking orders from these others that are having the disagreement. One of them goes with him, and there appears to be some kind of difficulty. The ones that were having the disagreement were like the leaders, and this Being was also one of the leaders. He flew the vessel, and one of the leaders flew with him and gave him instructions

116

which went against the general consensus. He pushed the ship too much, and it exploded.

Evelyn: Was Ed the pilot?

Athor: Yes.

Evelyn: The person with him gave him instructions and they were against what some of the other people thought would be the best thing to do; correct?

Athor: Yes. From that cycle the consciousness did not immediately go into any type of form. It appears to be lingering out in space, so to speak, in an amorphous shape. It was sort of hanging out there for a while because it wasn't in any great hurry to go into any other form after that particularly unpleasant experience. It sort of hung out as a consciousness in space, and basically it studied. This energy finally merged with certain systems, and then drew back into itself and merged over here (moves hand to the left) just to more or less get a feel for things in a formless state. It was a consciousness, an energy, and it wished to experience what various systems and energies were like.

Now we have a scene where there is a life form that is either trapped or is subterranean. We see a Being that has a metallic-looking skin type thing. The Being is putting something down the shaft, and there are pulses going through of some type. We are not sure if it is electromagnetic or what it is, but there are some tones. Evidently this shaft is one of many, and there is an underground tunnel system where these creatures live, and some go way down under there. There are different heights and levels to these tunnel systems.

117

This Being we are looking at is sending these pulses through there and is able to read, basically, the structure of this tunnel system, the depths and the different chambers, etc. but the pulses that are being put through are very irritating to the life form under there. It is upsetting all of their own sonar-type radar systems of that species.

There is a very distinct purpose to sending these pulses through there, not simply just to find the structure of the tunnel. They are looking for one shaft that they haven't found on the surface. It appears to be covered on the surface, and this one shaft seems to be important. It is an entry way into a greater tunnel system that goes very deep down. There is another life form in this other shaft. This life form is somehow connected with the life form that sent the pulses through. These two life forms have had some difficulty in the past. But this particular Being wants to make contact because there is someone of this other life form that the Being knows, and he wants to find the entrance and go through to find this Being. This other system of tunnels is almost like what might be termed the inner Earth. It is a whole different civilization, not like the creatures looking for this entrance.

Evelyn: (This is so bizarre that I am totally confused!) Is Ed the one sending the tones?

Athor: It would have to be. We do not see any other life form like that one at the moment.

Evelyn: So he is some sort of scientist?

Athor: Yes, but he has a personal reason.

Evelyn: Okay, what happens next?

Athor: The being that he was looking for is the one that was his most recent former wife. Evidently they went way back as souls in their encounters, and he was looking for that being. It was either a war or something that went on, and these beings developed this underground civilization. They had acclimated to living underground. It wasn't dark. They had a very sophisticated system under there so they were very much like this life form that the Ed being was except they lived under the surface.

Evelyn: Can you tell what planet or star system this was on?

Athor: It seems to go toward the Alpha Centauri system. But it does not look like this Being Edwin was actually living near there; not on the surface of that system or in the vicinity. It appears that he might be living elsewhere. He went partly because of the research, but then he had his own reasons to do this. When he did find the being he found the civilization to be very peaceful. The beings were friendly, but they did not wish any further contact with his group because there had been some kind of war way back when. It would appear that the war occurred not in the life cycle of the Ed Being and the other Being, but in their parent's time. We see that this Being, when he was very young somehow met the other Being. There was a great friendship and a bond that was established, and he wished to find this Being again.

Evelyn: Did the Being Lindy stay there underground?

Athor: Yes, although the Ed Being stayed some time there, but when it was found that she would not come

119

forth from there, he left with great regrets. But he had a life to go back to.

Lindy was Ed's Lt. Colonel wife. In another reading Athor had given a long story about her saving Ed's life, rescuing and nursing him back to health. In this lifetime Lindy had cancer for about ten years after they were married, so it was his turn to nurse her and attend to her needs. The bond between these two was obviously very deep, as reflected in Ed's insistence on continuing with setting up a scholarship program in Lindy's honor at Fresno State University. I went along with this, mainly because I recognized the deep soul bonds the two shared from past lives.

Evelyn: Do you see any lifetimes Off-Earth between Evelyn and Ed?
Athor: We have here a scene where there are two Beings. These are of a tall variety, but they are not as thin as the other ones we spoke of. They appear to be more substantially built in structure. Besides being tall, they don't look as rubbery, shall we say. These two Beings are communicating. It appears to be some kind of family situation. They are related somehow. It is not just co-workers or scientific. The sexes of this group were not clearly defined, having the potentiality of both sexes. They had the capacity to bring forth one gender, so to speak, over another. They would more or less take turns in doing this, so it wasn't a fixed thing that one was male and one was female. Each of them had the complete abilities of both sexes, and would just modulate depending on many factors, whatever was going on. Generally, they were more or less

androgynous in their normal functioning in sort of day-to-day routines, but when they found a Being that they were compatible with, then this aspect would come forth and they would play with that, and take turns. So this is what we see between these two, why there appears to be a partnership situation with these two. It appears that in that cycle they had a lifetime commitment, so to speak, although it is different than humans obviously; but there appears to be a working together of the energies in that cycle.

Evelyn: I assume there were children, if you could call them that.

Athor: There was no procreation through those forms. They were created, almost engineered. There was something that was added from the two Beings, but the Beings themselves through their forms did not give birth. They were engineered.

Evelyn: What system was this?

Athor: This is a system which has not been named. It is near Polaris, the North Star.

Evelyn: Is there a sort of pattern of the Off-Earth lives, because it looks like there were a variety of existences. Is there anything Off-Earth that relates to his strong interest in the military?

Athor: The Ed being has had a number of cycles of simply studying different things, curiosity, wanting to understand, wanting to learn, wanting to know more. There is no set pattern, per se, except the desire to learn. That has been brought through from Off-Earth cycles as well. The military situation appears primarily to have come from the Earth base life cycles, as we see there have been many, many cycles for this Being wherein he was in some type of military situation for many centuries.

Evelyn: Are there any particular countries where he has spent a number of lifetimes?

Athor: It would appear he was in the European sector. The Being has spent considerable time in the area of the Balkans, also Spain, Morocco and some other parts of Africa that are on the ocean, not inland. It is not like the Being has been in every country in the world in past cycles, but there have been cycles in the Great Pyrenees, parts of South America, the Yucatan Peninsula and the western part of the United States, as well as one or two cycles near the Bering Straits.

Evelyn: What about England? Ed has always felt a very strong affinity for this country.

Athor: Some.

Evelyn: Sweden? Lindy was Swedish and he loved visiting her relatives in Sweden.

Athor: Not too many; not like hundreds.

Evelyn: Can you get any information as to why the Ed Soul would choose to be born into a family composed of people who have given him little but negative experiences?

Athor: These Beings, each in their own right and way, had life cycles with the Ed Being that were unresolved. By that we mean that the scales were topped to where the Ed Being was more in control of certain situations. And these Beings felt each individually in different circumstances that they had been wronged in past cycles. They did not seek to make amends because they felt that they had been wronged in past cycles. So in this cycle they carried on the tradition, so to speak.

The best thing that the Ed Being can do in this situation is to go deep within and forgive, to allow them to be who they are.

To allow them to be who they are, however difficult and heart breaking that is, that is the advice because it is seen that these Beings are on their own track, and they will not readily change. Rather than carrying this karma on into further cycles, it is best to forgive and release, because they will carry their own stuff on; but he should not carry the burden of their karma. They have many lessons to learn. They are in some ways not as evolved as the Being Ed. They still have quite a ways to go. And there can be little done except to forgive. Bless them within, send prayers, send light and accept the fact that they simply are going their own way. That is not the path that his Being is on. They have many, many issues that they hold onto very strongly. The Ed energy is more like a vast field. It is contained, but there is a greater energy framework of the Ed Being.

Now these other beings are each like small units of energy that are very tightly compacted, and they are compartmentalized. They become very rigid and they can't let go. So here with Ed, we have a more expanded energy that has the capacity within that sphere to get on with it, because he is more advanced. It is his karmic lesson to forgive, to bless, and to let go. They cannot. On the ethers they cannot until a higher form of energy comes in and blesses them, releases them, and allows that energy to flow.

It would seem that Ed released a great deal of karma in this lifetime, as reflected in the Athor reading after he passed over into the higher realms. He had four children. Only his son and his family attended his Masonic service and burial in Arlington. I regrettably never met any of his daughters. He very much would have liked to have seen them again before he died, but they seemingly had no interest in seeing him.

Colonel Edwin Cook's funeral procession at Arlington, VA

I was trustee for Ed's trust; therefore, most of my time for almost two years was occupied dealing with his barn, property, vehicles, etc. All of these things needed to be disposed of or sold, since his estate was left to Fresno State University for the Cook Endowed Scholarship for nurses. When I met Ed he was very involved with setting up this scholarship, and that meant many trips down to Fresno State. There are two beautiful display cabinets in the nursing department, with uniforms and various items from the military careers of Ed and his late wife, Lt. Colonel Elvera Cook. I heard a great deal about Lindy (as Elvera was known), and must say that I found it difficult to attend the event in 2010 honoring Ed for his large contribution to the university.

The president of Fresno State presented me with a very beautiful crystal obelisk, with Ed's name engraved on the base. At the reception, prior to his presentation on the stage, I met many of the leaders of Fresno State. Since Ed had left his entire estate to the scholarship fund to honor himself and Lindy, as I sat on the stage, I felt it was an awkward situation. I kept thinking that everyone I met was speculating on how I felt about honoring Ed's late wife. I can't honestly say I had no resentment about all of Ed's money going toward the scholarship, but many students will be helped in the future, and I became good friends with the Director of Planned Giving. He and his wife treated me like royalty during my stay in Fresno.

I received a very nice note from the Director of the Nursing Department, giving me the names of the three students who will be taking advantage of the Cook Scholarship in the Fall of 2011. At this point, I am delighted that so many students will be assisted in their education. The scholarship is in perpetuity, so will be ongoing for many years to come.

Chapter 11

Ed's UFO Experience

Colonel Cook - F94 Korea.

Very soon after meeting Ed he noted my many books about UFO's, extraterrestrials, etc. which led him to tell me about his encounter with a UFO while flying in Korea. I suggested a hypnotic session to see what else he could remember about the incident but there was little more to the story than he had already told me. However, what was apparent was the extreme fear he felt during this experience. He was in an F- 94 night fighter which had been on patrol one night when suddenly he noticed a tremendous white light following the plane. They couldn't get away from it, nor could they identify whatever was projecting this almost blinding light. He said it was as if it was playing with them. This lasted for quite some time, and then suddenly it was gone. He was soaking wet with perspiration, even though the cockpit was quite cold. This happened in 1952, but he still remembered the incident quite vividly. After reporting it, he was later flown to Japan to be debriefed. After Ed and I had talked about this, I suggested he look up Project Blue Book on the Internet, and found that this was one of unexplained cases of unidentified flying objects.

From UFO US Military Reports, Korea, 1952:
In June 1952 the Air Force was taking the UFO problem seriously. One of the reasons was that there were a lot of good UFO reports coming in from Korea. Fighter pilots reported seeing silver colored spheres or disks on several occasions, and radar in Japan, Okinawa, and in Korea had tracked unidentified targets. (Captain Edward J Ruppelt, head of Project Blue Book, in his book, *The Report on Unidentified Flying Objects*.)
On May 31, 1952, at 3:45 local time, a Lockheed F-94 Starfire fighter pilot of the 319th fighter squadron, based at Suwon Air Base encountered a UFO over Korea in the South of Chorwon. It was both radar and visual sighting, which later was recorded in ufologist Dominique Weinstein's catalog of UFO/Aircraft

encounters. The pilot reported one white-bluish round object, tracked on airborne radar, not on ground radar. First, the object was sighted by ground witnesses. The pilot of the F-94 tracked on his radar and saw a round, brilliant, bluish-white light. According to the pilot's statement: "On May 31st, 1952, the F-94 descended in a port turn to intercept an unidentified object 6,000 feet below, on a 90 degree turn course and at an altitude of 8,000 ft. The UFO began a port climb at the same time to intercept the descending F-94, and accomplished a maneuver which silhouetted the F-94 against the light of dawn. The F-94 turned on its afterburner and tried two quartering head-on passes with the UFO, resulting in neither being able to get astern of the other. The pilot's maneuvers ensued to 3,000 feet where more passes were exchanged for a few minutes. The UFO then increased its speed to an estimated 400 knots on a 45 degree heading, and began pulling away from the F-94. When last seen, the UFO had seemingly increased its speed to approximately 450 knots, where upon the F-94 gave up pursuit at 3:55 AM and returned to base."

When it was assigned the first three all new F-94 all-weather interceptor jets, the 319th became the first all-weather fighter-interceptor squadron of the Air Force. The "all-weather" qualification also means that the aircraft is equipped with on-board radar. The 319th DIS was deployed to Korea because it was the most experienced with the F-94.

There was certainly no question about Ed's belief in UFOs after experiencing this incident so we had this belief system in common. Unfortunately the Air Force still seems to be denying the existence of UFOs. An extensive article was written by John T. Correll in the June 2011 Air Force Journal regarding his research on the UFO issue. He cited many cases, and I was pleased that he had conducted such supposedly thorough research. However, he concluded by basically negating that they exist, even though he stated that polls find more than half of the adult American population believes the government is concealing information about UFOs, and almost half of the public believes that aliens have visited the Earth.

John Correll was editor in chief of Air Force Magazine for 18 years and is now a contributing editor. It no doubt is in his best interest to continue the cover-up, although it is interesting that mainly military personnel are the main readers of the magazine. This makes me wonder why he wrote the article at all!

In the next issue of Air Force Times there were several Letters to the Editor commenting on the article written by Correll. I was pleased by a very interesting letter from Colonel David J. Shea, USAF (Ret.). It is a very long letter, but to quote the greatest problem in a nutshell: "Why Correll skirted the PR aspects of the UFO phenomenon is puzzling. The Air Force was its own worst enemy, for the story of the Air Force and UFOs is essentially a tale of a credibility gap wider than the Grand Canyon. In the final analysis, it was the Air Force's unwillingness to be open and frank with the press and public about UFOs that caused the service more than 20 years of grief."

Chapter 12

Ed's Near-Death Experience

Bandon Sunset

The second fascinating story about Ed was his near death experience. He was alone at home on his ranch not long after Lindy had died of cancer. He was very depressed, when suddenly he couldn't see out of his right eye and had a feeling that he was dying. His thought was, "So be it", but he asked God to give him some more time to accomplish some things he still wanted to do. To his knowledge, he lost consciousness after that, and the next thing he remembered was being outside the next morning about 10:00 AM. He was laying cinder blocks on something he had been building beside his house. It was then he noticed he could not see much out of his right eye and thought he might be having a stroke, so he got in his car and drove to Travis Air Force Base to see a doctor (about an hour's drive away through Sacramento traffic!)

They did extensive tests, but said he had not had a stroke; his vision had cleared up by then so he came on back home and seemed to be all right. What puzzled him was what happened between the time he blacked out the evening before and the time when he was laying blocks. He had no conscious memory of that period of time. Again we were not able to get any further explanation through a hypnosis session, so we decided to ask Athor about this. She said that it was like a near death experience; a higher aspect of Ed's soul had come in during that time, and his body was on automatic pilot when he was laying blocks. It would appear that he had been doing that for several hours before he actually had some memory of what had happened.

According to James Salz M.D. of the University of Southern California, a sudden loss of vision could mean that you are about to have a stroke. Patients may experience an almost total loss of vision in one eye caused by cholesterol plaque in the carotid artery in the neck. The loss of central vision is known as amaurosis fugax. Normal vision returns when the cholesterol deposit passes through, usually within a few minutes. In Ed's case we assume that this is what happened and he blacked out. What had continued to puzzle him was how he could have been laying blocks the next morning when he returned to consciousness.

When he drove himself to the Travis Air Force Base Hospital, the doctors could find no evidence of a stroke, so he really never knew what happened medically. I asked him if he felt very different after that. He stated that his depression lifted and he decided to get on with his life which included going on a cruise to Europe and having a wonderful time. I thought it likely I would not have really been attracted to Ed before this change in his psyche. Athor had given a rather long description which I never had transcribed, but the bottom line was it was a gift from his soul to help him heal from the trauma of Lindy's death.

Chapter 13

Ed's Messages from the Other Side

Ed and University Staff in front of Cook Memorial Displays

After Ed's transition, I felt a strong need to communicate with him. This began a series of readings with Aki. She is no longer Athor but now channels Athor. This chapter covers those transmissions.

First contact: May 23, 2009 (sixteen days after Ed's transition from the Earth plane) Athor states that three Beings of Light took Ed into the Light. Ed was confused and in danger of being stuck on the Earth plane, since he was concerned about leaving me. (Athor, along with her friend Lydia, had prayed for Ed's release into The Light). This message took quite a while, since Athor said she was bathing in the beauty of these Beings of Light.

It sounded quite wonderful from her description, although I was not able to see any of this. Finally, Athor told me that Ed had taken a great step forward in his evolution. The energy he is in now is quite beautiful, a wonderful energy (she was still enjoying this energy!) Ed is open to new ideas, very different from his mind set here on Earth. He burned off a great deal of karma (through difficult family relationships and many physical problems); being exposed to my metaphysical beliefs prepared the way for him to be open to these new energies. There has been a cutoff of his Earthly ties, which explained to me my deep depression the last few days. His energy has completely left me.

Second contact: June 6, 2009 (thirty days after his transition) Ed has gone to a new level. He is balancing the scales; looking at his lives past and present to see how well he has balanced karma. A Council is working with him to make tentative plans for his next lifetime. He will go through further stages at higher levels, but at this point he is reviewing and planning.

Third contact: June 18, 2009 (forty two days after transition) From an inner level, Ed was "bursting to get loose" from his physical body (Ed had prostate cancer, his kidneys had shut down, etc. - his body was no longer serving him in any productive way). He couldn't wait to get on with it. (Ed was a 50 year plus Mason who believed in a Supreme Being, and he thought he believed in reincarnation.) Ed's spirit was flying in a realm checking out other realms that are not on Earth. (He loved flying and was an excellent pilot. When we both knew that his death was eminent, I had commented to him, "Just think, you will be able to fly again.") Ed will wake up to a certain level later on, but his consciousness is geared toward the experiences he is having now.

July 25, 2009 there was a Masonic Memorial Service for Ed in Bandon, conducted by the local Masonic Lodge. It was a very beautiful service but I did not feel Ed's presence. Perhaps the deceased person attends the service if it is held soon after death when the spirit is still on the Earth plane. Since Ed had been a Mason in California, and had not actually joined the lodge in Bandon, I had to find evidence that he was actually a Mason, plus the current Masonic Master wanted to see Ed's Masonic apron, and I had great difficulty finding that. It, therefore, took a lot of time and planning before we could actually have the Memorial service, a request of Ed's in addition to wanting the full military service at Arlington.

Fourth contact: August 23, 2009 (more than three months since his transition.) Ed regrets many things he did. Now he is just going with the flow; he has no control over anything (as a colonel Ed liked to be in control, so this was quite different for him.) He is confused but not afraid – there is nothing to be afraid of. I wanted to know what he had thought about the Masonic service. His only comment was that he liked the ritual. I sensed that he was really detached from what was happening at the service, but of course, there is a very standard ritual used for all such funerals, and it is quite impressive. I then wanted to know if he had met Lindy, his deceased wife, on the other side. He said that he has had fleeting encounters with her. I had thought this would be a grand reunion, but it didn't sound that way! Athor stated that everyone's death experience is unique. It is not like a welcoming committee.

I then asked if we would meet again. He answered, "Yes, do not grieve for me. It is worse for those who are left behind in a body (Ed and I had talked about this since we both had lost former spouses to cancer.) I kept trying to find out how Ed could communicate directly with me rather than through Athor. He said he will try, but he is not sure how to get through the denseness to communicate. Athor described this denseness in terms of air currents, turbulence, etc. - terms that a pilot such as Ed would use.

This session with Ed seemed to be more of the judgment phase after death. "I had quite a temper. I did a lot of things that were wrong." From my point of view Ed was an extremely moral man, but he tended to look at things in black and white, with little middle ground. He apparently did have a temper, although I observed little of this during our marriage. Ed was the President of the Air Force Association in Sacramento. He held monthly meetings at the Sacramento Convention Center. Speakers were usually well known generals. Ed had been on the list to become a general, but he had a disagreement with the local general at the former McClellan Air Force Base. The Air Force meetings had always been held on base at the Officers Club. The general demanded that they remain at this location, but Ed refused because he wanted the meetings to be more accessible to the public. His late wife, a Lt. Colonel, told Ed that you don't talk to a general like that! After that incident, Ed was removed from the prospective general's list.

Perhaps Ed was recalling experiences similar to this. He said he guessed he would reincarnate, but it may be some other form rather than human. He added that he guessed there is a hell, but it is not what people think it is. I have no idea why he made the comment about hell unless he was still judging himself more than less evolved beings might do, and this was his hell. Apparently being on the other side certainly does not give one all the answers.

Fifth contact: October 7, 2009 (five months after transition) Ed is feeling a great deal of freedom. There are open hills, and he can see for many miles. He has dropped the Earth personality, so it would be difficult for a medium to contact him. I had contacted another psychic who supposedly could communicate with those who have crossed over, but she had great difficulty even finding Ed. Most of what she said didn't ring a bell with me. She was a nice lady, and seemed very frustrated because she couldn't answer my questions. Earlier Athor had said she thought that most mediums who contact the deceased were reading energies from the lower astral level. It would seem that Ed had progressed further than that.

On September 7, 2009, I had a very strange, involved dream which was quite vivid. The main theme seemed to be that I was trying to reach Ed on my cell phone, but couldn't dial his number. I kept trying to figure out some way to call him, and then I woke up. It had occurred to me that maybe Ed would try to reach me on my cell phone, but I forgot about this.

Through a stress test and an angiogram I discovered I had some heart blockages, and that resulted in my having three stents inserted into my heart. The doctors were rather insistent that I have bypass surgery, but I was equally insistent that I was soon flying to Washington to attend my late husband's memorial service at Arlington National Cemetery. Although it was a difficult trip, I was thankful that there were no major health incidents.

I was once again grateful to be back in my home in Bandon. There had been a five months lapse from the time Ed passed over to his burial at Arlington. There had been much planning involved in his service, and there were many others on the Arlington list ahead of Ed. Also, October is a lovely month in Washington, with the leaves turning many colors. Relatives and friends from all over the country were attending, and they all needed lead time to plan their schedules.

In a later reading in December I asked Athor/Aki to find out what Ed thought about his Arlington service. Unfortunately she said there is not much energy connected with the Earth at that point, but he liked the military procession and the horses (Athor asked me later if there were horses - she had no knowledge of military services.) There were indeed six beautiful white horses. She said that he also felt some energy directed toward me. He was gratified by the service and felt it was a good closing chapter to his life. I was rather disappointed in this reaction, since I thought it was a wonderful tribute to him. Apparently he was more interested at that point in what he was doing in the other realms. The feeling was still like being free - doing acrobatics in a plane. At that point he had no real concern for Earthly things.

When Ed was a cadet pilot in World War II he would often fly under bridges which was against regulations; but he loved doing it. Even though I had told him that when he was no longer in a body he could fly again, he didn't quite believe that. He says he has seen "The Light". He knows his attachment to material possessions was an imbalance in this lifetime (as mentioned before, Ed had lots of "stuff.")

There was a huge revelation soon after crossing over. Athor was about to conclude this reading when she said, "Wait, there is more. I see a red ball of light, and I'm trying to read the energy." This took quite a while, so I waited patiently. Finally, she said he is trying to warn of a pending war. "There will be between 20 and 40 nations involved -

military encounters, and global catastrophe. She said, "I hear 1978; does that mean anything to you?" It meant nothing to me nor to her, but when I looked it up on the Internet there were many alarming events in 1978, including the year that the Shah was deposed in Iran, which led to Ayatollah Khomeini returning to power; the Iranian hostage situation; the near Three Mile Island nuclear disaster, etc.

Ed said that the course of history can be substantially altered through prayer and sending Light. From his present prospective, Ed has seen what energies, thought waves and thought forms can do. During his last days on Earth Ed was extremely concerned about the situation on Earth. While on heavy pain medication he thought he was being called up again to help his country. Maybe the only way he can assist is from the other side. There will be much more about this later.

Back to the cell phone dream - Right before Christmas I had a really weird call on my cell phone. There was a great deal of static, then a voice was heard for a few seconds, but I could not understand what was being said. It finally dawned on me to call the telephone number that left the message. It turned out be from Lakeside, a community north of Bandon which borders on a large lake. The call was made from McKay's Market, a grocery store near the lake. The lady I talked with denied any knowledge of anyone calling my number in Bandon. As I considered all of this and remembered my dream, I realized that this must have been a call from Ed. He loved fishing, and had great pleasure eating before he became too ill to eat. It seemed quite appropriate that his spirit would try to send a message using the telephone at a grocery store near a large lake! If you watch Ghost Busters on television, you can believe that spirits often use electronic devices to send messages. Since I had never been to Lakeside I decided later to check it out. I found McKay's Market but before I went in I asked the man parked beside me if there was a lake nearby. Amazingly he was an Air Force veteran so we had an interesting conversation. I wanted to mention the telephone call but decided he might think I was delusional so I just went on into the grocery store where I simply looked around. From there I drove down the street to the location of a very large lake. I still feel that the strange voice on the telephone was an attempt by Ed to communicate with me.

In addition to this, strange things had been happening to the lights at my home. The light at the head of my bed kept turning on and off without my touching it. I thought maybe it needed a new bulb, but when I changed it, the same thing happened. I finally put the old bulb back in and it worked fine. Then the overhead lights in the garage would not turn on. The next day the lights came on as soon as I touched the switch.

I am basically a skeptic so I decided to check with Athor (Aki,) and she confirmed that indeed the phone call and light phenomena were the work of Ed. She also said that she had received a "message" from Ed saying that he was trying to communicate with me. That same night on the radio there was a man named "Cook" talking about electronic voices from the dead. Coincidence? I think not! For many months I continued to get phone calls on my land line, but there was no one there when I answered the calls. During a later Athor/Aki reading I asked more about Ed's possible direct communication with me:

Athor: Communication with the living can be a seasonal thing, depending on the weather. Rain and water can create a lot of so-called paranormal activity. For some reason, that is a little easier on the ethers. It thins them out - the difference between this realm and the next, so to speak. When it is foggy, damp or rainy; even snow can help with that. There are certain times of the year when the ethers are thinner, as well as certain places in the world where this is true; there is much more paranormal activity in countries such as Brazil and India. New Age people talk about psychic hot spots, because there are places in the world where the veil is thinner, so to speak.

Chapter 14

Ed's Warning of a Pending War

Ed in Air Force Dress

Sixth contact - December, 2009: Toward the end of Ed's last message he began talking about a pending war, but gave no details. He also added that we could change this by turning to "The Light" (same as God, All That Is, etc.)

Evelyn: Is there any Earth time line about when this might be happening, and if our consciousness can change it?

Athor/Aki: (Ed through Athor/Aki) Two to three years.

Evelyn: Would this be through an atomic explosion, or something else?

Athor/Aki: I don't have that knowledge. It's the political climate of a domino effect that will occur.

Evelyn: Is there anything specifically that we can do to help prevent this, other than prayer and sending Light? Are there any individuals I should contact?

Athor/Aki: What I am hearing, the powers to be have determined certain events will occur within a certain time frame. These events can only be circumvented through the use of Light, a sufficient number of Beings joining together, uniting, and the right individual taking necessary steps. It is unlikely that such individuals would be open-minded enough to believe Ed's transmission. It is a giant leap from the material in *From Sirius to Earth* to the political arena. Most of these individuals are not able to make that leap. They have no framework – no basis. They have to be approached on their level, in their language, is what I am getting.

When Ed and I were at dinner parties with people who have no metaphysical background he would often say, "Tell them about your book, Evelyn." I would usually be at a loss to explain it in a way that would make any sense to them. Then Ed would often tell them that it explains the Universe, and the good Lord has a lot of help (referring of course to the Council of Sirius.) The subject would then be quickly dropped because our friends, mainly Ed's retired military friends, could not even think of any questions or polite comments!

I was not willing to post the following information on my website back in December 2009. However, considering all the Earth events since then, perhaps the time has come when this information should be made public.

It was not until April 2010 that I finally made the decision to send the information from Ed to someone in a leadership position. Aside from the pending war, another shocking message was that Ed was preparing for his rebirth. This is a very involved process that I will address later, but it was clear that I was not going to receive any additional information regarding the world crisis, since all of his energies were going toward the rebirth process. I was not pleased at all over his choice. He was planning to be born in Libya to a Muslim family. Athor said Ed's leadership abilities would carry over into the next lifetime, although the personality would be quite different. His soul must have felt that he would be needed there. This was well over a year before all of the fighting broke out in Libya.

On April 3, 2010 I wrote a letter to the general in charge of the U.S. African Command. It was an APO address, which I recall, was a location in Germany. At any rate, I never received a reply or any acknowledgement that he received it.

After the aborted attempt of an attack on New York City, US Attorney General Eric Holder was very much in the news; therefore, I wrote a somewhat amended letter to him. I still had the nagging feeling that Ed wanted this information to go to someone who was in a position to take some action. After giving Mr. Holder some of Ed's background, stating among other things, that he was buried with full military honors at Arlington. I then briefly talked about Athor, whom I described only as a psychic/mystic who was one of my former clients with whom I have had ongoing contact. I was attempting to sound very professional in the hope that Mr. Holder would not think I was some kind of nut! The following are parts of my letter, with various additional comments from me:

> After my husband Ed passed away I wanted to see if I could contact him via Athor. The first contact was May 23 2009, sixteen days after his death. These contacts continued periodically; then on December 11, 2009, suddenly Athor stated that Ed was trying to warn of a pending war. There will be between 20-30 nations involved – military encounters, and global catastrophe. Ed was giving a date of 1978, which meant nothing to Athor or to me, but after doing some research I concluded that this was the beginning of the roots of this pending war. It was the year that the Shah of Iran was deposed, which led to Ayatollah Khomeini returning to power, as well as many other chaotic events. I feel that giving this date was Ed's way of convincing Athor and me that the information was indeed coming from him. Ed had been an avid student of history, so was well versed in world events. Despite my metaphysical work, I tend to be a skeptic, and I really didn't want to believe anything Ed was telling me.
>
> Now as to why I am contacting you, Mr. Holder, Ed stated that the war would begin in Algiers. This was a shock since I had not heard anything lately about any particular problems there, but according to information on the Internet, there have been

continuing terrorist activities, although it has not been prominent in the news as much as the other African hotspots. I have no idea what you can do with this information, but I feel sure Ed brought this through because he was extremely concerned about the Earth situation, and wanted me to pass this information along to someone who might be in a position to utilize it, or pass it on to someone else you trust who would possibly be able to do something about these problems. The problems are so wide spread that it is really more of an intelligence issue, not anything that the U.S. alone can do anything about. I have frankly been in a dilemma about what to do with the information. My inclination has been to do nothing, but Ed served in the military for 40 years, attended War College, etc. and I sense that he very much wants me to pass this on to someone in authority.

So this is from Ed: "There is a strong energy of tremendous clashes and negativity in the Middle East area (this was no surprise to me). Saudi Arabia is a problem because of their underground connections. There is some kind of terrorist cell in Spain that needs to be located. They are infiltrating certain European countries, little by little like a cancer spreads. There are remote pockets in other parts of the world that are not necessarily connected to these terrorist groups. These local types of activities are in certain countries due to their own factions and energy. There is a stronger entity from the Middle East in some countries more than others.

"There is a small faction in France, Belgium and Germany. Antwerp, Belgium particularly needs to be looked at, and Frankfort, Germany, the Palisades in New Jersey (this certainly shocked me). Spain keeps coming up. There is a growing element in that country; it is not the government, per se, but a geographical location. For some reason they are trying to set up a real strong type of base there. Perhaps they are actually either training or planning on training people there. I don't know, but there is something very strong coming up with that country."

Ed is saying that Israel must be watched because it is a real time bomb. They may take matters into their own hands; they don't like to be told anything that is recommended. He is indicating that Israel is a hot bed of instability, although it is not a terrorist network. (I should comment that Ed and I had a number of good Jewish friends, so there is no element of prejudice in his remarks, just the situation as he sees it.)

While in War College, Ed had to write a long paper on campaigns. I asked him if he were in charge what kind of strategy would he use.

There are strategies and campaigns where you do the same things in 15 to 25 places almost simultaneously and sometimes like a chain reaction. Athor says she hears counter- it is a counter offense, a counter attack, and disburse. You rush in and you disperse the so-called enemy. It is almost guerrilla warfare, only a lot more complex. It involved coming into a central position and making the energy disperse by whatever means. So whether it is through bombing or some other form of attack/infiltration - these are all forms and methods that can be used to get them to disperse so they are no longer united, and have no central core. Many of the cells are being funded through Saudi Arabia, and that energy line connects to Spain, funded through European banks. There are three separate factions - three arms to their whole plan. The third is not yet fully operational, but two are pretty well established. That doesn't mean that the individual cells are fully functional, but it means the roots have been made. They seek to engage the whole world in war. That is their aim. Al-Qaeda is only one of the factions (Ed was 84 when he died, so attended War College many years ago. I realize strategies have changed a great deal since then, but I thought I would include this just in case it has any value at the present time.)

I asked the question, "Is Osama bin Laden a key factor in any of this at this time?" He kind of oversees certain developments, but there are many other people that have come forth and he has put them in a position of power. The ones that are carrying these things out are the ones in positional power. The whole issue with Osama is veiled. It is hard to say if he is definitely in power, but he has a lot of people in a few countries. He is very well protected. This information is from December 11, 2009, and was obviously transmitted before the raid on the house in Pakistan by the Navy Seals in which Osama was killed in May, 2011. Hopefully, the confiscated material will give locations and names of these other Al-Qaeda leaders.

I hate to lay this on you, Mr. Holder, because it is obviously very complicated. Considering the attempted attacks on New York City, the part of this that mainly concerns me is Ed's mentioning the New Jersey Palisades. He gave no details on this, but perhaps you know something about that area. There apparently will be no more military information coming from Ed. If this were strictly information from a psychic, I certainly would not be contacting people in the government. As stated, my main goal in contacting Ed was to be sure he was thriving on the other side after his Earth transition. Giving this kind of information regarding the earth situation, a pending war, etc., was quite unnerving to me.

I have a website, www.evelynfuqua.com, where I have been posting all of the contacts with Ed, but I have been afraid frankly to include any of this information I am sending to you. I am hoping by the time this book is published, the political situations in Africa and the Middle East will have settled down. Since bin Laden is no longer a threat, only time will tell whether this information is valid and/or can be useful to our leaders.

In an effort to be sure Attorney General Holder read my letter I sent it registered mail. The receipt was returned with someone's signature, so I can only assume that the letter was given to Eric Holder. I had mentioned in my letter to him that there was a problem in the New Jersey Palisades area. Several weeks after that, I was reading my local Coos Bay, Oregon paper that stated that two men from the New Jersey Palisades area were arrested as they were headed to the airport to seek terror training from Al-Qaeda affiliated jihadists. Although I never received any reply from Mr. Holder, I am guessing that my letter gave him enough impetus to go after these young men who apparently had been watched and suspected for several months.

Several of my military friends suggested I send a letter to Secretary of State Hilary Clinton, which I finally did. Once again, I sent it certified mail with a return receipt, but there was no direct contact with Hilary Clinton. I guess the government can't acknowledge that they received accurate information from a psychic! My only goal was to do something to help with the war on terror through the messages from my Colonel husband.

I have continued to wonder about Ed's reference to Algeria. In doing recent research on this area I learned that all three of the people to whom I sent a letter have had close connections with Algeria: the American General in charge of the African sector visited with Algerian officials including President Bouteflika in November 2009; Eric Holder signed the Mutual Legal Assistance Treaty with Algerian Justice Minister Tayeb Belaiz on April 2010; and Algerian Foreign Minister Medelci met with Secretary Hilary Clinton in Washington D. C. December 2009. Ed's message about a pending war was in late December 2009. Perhaps Ed was picking up on some of these visits from the ethers, although seemingly Algeria and the United States have a good relationship.

I was worried about Ed's over-concern (to my thinking) about this pending war situation. In a February 10 reading in 2010, I asked if Ed can do anything from his side to help this situation.

He replied (via Athor,) not much, other than trying to give information of what he sees and what he is aware of. The rest of the reading was devoted to asking if Ed had a message for our friend Pam, who is Chief of Staff for a Congressman, and had orchestrated Ed's burial in Arlington from her office in

Cosmic Relationships

Washington D.C. Athor's comment ended up going into a rather involved past life they (Ed and Pam) had together when they were friends in the days of the Old West. Pam felt a close bond with Ed, and has missed him almost as much as I have.

It is almost Veteran's Day 2011 and the world situation seems to be changing almost daily. I still have no idea if any of this information is valid. It is my hope that the individuals in leadership positions took this seriously enough to at least look into some of these possibilities. If in fact they did, and with the assistance of the millions of people who have now raised their consciousness at this time in our evolution, hopefully we will have no more major wars.

Chapter 15

Ed's Rebirth on Planet Earth

Bandon Sunrise

I was still concerned about Ed's pending rebirth in Libya. I became increasingly concerned when all of the fighting broke out in that country in 2011. Prior to that as a metaphysician I was quite fascinated by the whole planning of a rebirth. Athor had indicated there could be no forthcoming information about the pending war situation so I decided to totally drop that as a line of questioning. The following is the beginning of my hearing about Ed's rebirth via an Athor reading regarding Ed on March, 22, 2010:

Evelyn: See where Ed is and what the situation is with him before we try to ask any questions.

Athor: One moment. It is seen that the energy has contracted. There is this balling of energy and it has contracted into – I don't know if it is a physical fetus or if it's in the entrance stage where it is amassing the energies and collecting the energies. It has contracted and collected the energies into a small base, so to speak.

Evelyn: Is there anything we can even ask him with that situation or could I go to you Athor to get some information about other things. Should I even try to ask him? I don't want to disturb this birth process.

Athor: No, I don't think so because there is too much - the energy is collected and concentrated in a pre-birth pattern, I hear.

Evelyn: My goodness (I have no idea another birth would be so soon. This is less than a year since his transition) Can you find out where he will incarnate?

Athor: I hear Libya.

Evelyn: (Big shock!!) Can you find out why he wants to incarnate in Libya?

Athor: I hear there is much work to be done.

Keep in mind this was long before the bloody uprisings in Libya in 2011.

Evelyn: Will he be born as a baby or could he possibly be a Walk-In?

Athor: A baby.

Evelyn: Can you find out anything about his parents?

Athor: Well, they won't be of the poor class. They are not like billionaire types, but they are well off, educated. Have some kind of political ties. They may be a prominent family with political ties.

Evelyn: Do they have any connections to al Qaeda?

Athor: Yes and no.

Evelyn: What does that mean?

Athor: Connections in a sense in that they are well informed of some of the goings on. There are factions within that family unit that are indeed connected in a direct way. Whereas factions are just aware of goings on; they are not as directly connected. And he is going to be coming from the branch that is not directly connected, because there are just some shenanigans afoot to topple a regime.

Evelyn: I don't know anything about the leadership right now in Libya. I will have to see what I can find out. Can you get a location in Libya, a town, a city where his parents live? (Much discussion about this – I am sending Athor a map - still waiting to receive an answer on this.)

Evelyn: How many children are in the family?

Athor: It is one of those extended families – not as large as bin Laden's but a similar concept, where there are a lot of relatives. They don't have families like that here as a rule.

Evelyn: The family I presume will be Muslim? (The extended family would be the result of many wives with many children.)

Athor: Yes.

Evelyn: Are they strict Muslims according to their relationships with women and that kind of thing?

157

Athor: There are factions to this extended family. And I hear some are dyed in the wool strict Muslims and some are more liberal. This is part of the problem that he hopes to address with his incarnation along with other issues on the political front. Yes, but this is in the makings. And this thing about a political overthrow is in the works. (Remember, this reading was given March 22, 2010; the movement to overthrow Muammar el-Qaddafi was not until April, 2011.)

Evelyn: When Ed grows up, will he be in a leadership position in that country?

Athor: The answer is yes and no; leadership in terms of being singled out and known worldwide, no; leadership within the family unit and extended areas, yes.

Evelyn: Okay. So he can use some of the things he has learned spiritually to help the situation hopefully.

Athor: Yes. It is like it is saying that many, many jobs that the soul, the spirit, whatever comes to do are not necessarily pleasant. And, in that sense, the help that he will provide will have and does have ramifications and repercussions. It is like throwing a pebble in a pond and you see these concentric circles coming around it and widening out. This is what is seen, but the end result is positive. But in the meantime from the energies of the pebble the concentric circle widens, creating quite a stir and havoc in many systems and realms, and so forth. And, so, this child will have that effect.

Evelyn: This will be a male child then?

Athor: Yes.

Evelyn? In what Earth time frame then do you think he will actually be born? What astrological sign will he be born under?

Athor: There is a time frame in which the energies amass for a spirit and while it is amassing like that, there can be no disturbance. There will be no communication because it can't be pushed; that would be damaging to the incoming spirit and I don't quite know why. I have to study that one day. I had that happen with Leila (Athor's daughter.) I was seven months pregnant and I wanted to check in on what the spirit was like, and I was told in no uncertain terms, no because it would knock her out and a different spirit would come in. So I had to wait a month. So at eight months I could. Even in the non-physical realm this seems to apply. When the energies are amassing, it is almost as if the energy is picking the sperm that is going to be infiltrating the egg type of thing. So, there is a huge concentration of energies amassing on the so-called other side to get everything ready.

Evelyn: So the month and date of his birth we really can't get now?

Athor: This is not a haphazard thing. Each egg that is fertilized, that is planned, energetically, it all works together because, of course, the genetic components of an egg being fertilized by a particular sperm are very, very important. So we are looking at the whole phenomenon as an energy phenomenon. It isn't just a physical thing that the sperm penetrates a particular egg and there you have it. It is almost like a precise engineering process. If the energies are in the amassing stage, this process has not occurred. They have to amass.

There is a certain magnetic and balance energetic effort that is required between amassing the energies from the so-called other side and bridging the gap into this world - there is a very almost scientific process that is involved in that. It is not just that the energies amass and then are swooped into the womb. The being may experience that in its memory, but that is not the full process.

And so, Ed is in that process where the energies are amassing on the so-called other side to get ready to balance out the energies in this realm, to be able to come through and have the right sperm and egg and the whole bit. So, we are looking at a time period and this fluctuates; it is not set because there are a lot of factors involved, but we are looking at three or four months, possibly, before there is an actual embryo.

Evelyn: Is there any group or Being that is overseeing this whole process? Who are the supervisors of this?

Athor: There is no answer.

Evelyn: There is no answer?

Athor: No, there is just silence. So I could assume that it is not to be revealed at this time. Whoever or whatever these forces or whatever are, are not willing to divulge that at this time.

Evelyn: I am wondering if I go to Fresno State to accept the award for Ed's Nurses' Scholarship program, would that interfere with this amassing process that is happening. (Dumb question probably, but answer was interesting).

Athor: This amassing process is actually a different spirit that is being formed.

Evelyn: Please explain.

Athor: The soul remains, it doesn't incarnate. But it projects a spirit, and these spirits are different with each incarnation. The soul remains the same.

Evelyn: OK. In the Religious Research teachings that I had been following for many years prior to meeting you, the channel, Dr. John, talked about simply a different personality incarnating, but that is really the same thing as a different spirit isn't it?

Athor: The soul remains consistent from life to life from incarnation to incarnation because that is like the overseer of all the incarnations. The soul puts out a spirit for a particular incarnation that is formed, and it is saying that the spirit that represented that personality has dissolved.

Evelyn: So there would be no point in trying to have any contact or talk to him?

Athor: No, because the soul has gone on to a new phase, to a new existence.

Evelyn: What can you tell me about how he made the decision to incarnate in that particular country?

I asked this question before all of the present conflicts began in Libya — at least Athor had said that he was incarnating in the southeastern part of the country which would be away from the major fighting and bombing by NATO.

Athor: I hear the political realities of the times. When he physically died, and he did an overview of not only his life but in the realms that he visited, and learned

161

from, and traveled after his physical death, he saw the political realities of what was happening on this planet. He wanted to affect things and see where he could do the most good. That was the decision that was made, not from the human realm, but after he physically died. The consciousness made that decision. It was not so much his personality as Edwin Cook that made that decision, because that was already on its way out after he physically died.

Evelyn: Did he have any kind of soul committee or any helpers in making that decision, or was it totally a decision of his soul?

Athor: I hear that there is much dramatization on Planet Earth. The human beings put their own spin on that than what is really so. It doesn't happen the way that a lot of people say it happens. In certain instances, there are so many astral planes, first of all. They appear to be almost infinite, the astral planes. So when a being physically dies and the soul begins dissolving that spirit, the consciousness has experiences in various astral planes or astral realms. Depending on which of these planes or realms that the spirit is engaged in and is experienced in, that would determine whether they have this committee-type overview, and those types of experiences.

With Ed that was not so much the case. You know he went into different astral planes. As an example, when I was working with a man who was more or less possessed, I was shown some of the planes and dimensions that we worked on while he was physically alive, but traveled astrally. I was horrified because they were not realms I would want

162

to travel in. The energy was full of knives, glass shards and swords, not a nice place. Therefore, there are an infinite number of astral planes and realms that a being can go into after they physically die. Depending on which ones they are in will determine whether they have this life review with a committee of beings or take a different route. In Ed's case he didn't go into those places. He took a different route where he was observing what is happening here on Earth, and he desired to be of service in his next lifetime.

It had been increasingly difficult to receive any further information from Athor due to her progressing health issues but finally on May 16, 2011 she was able to give me Ed's date of birth. However, due to the continued political unrest in Libya and my concern for the safety of the child, I have decided it best to keep that information confidential. This was a very carefully planned rebirth. Unfortunately I doubt that this is the case with all births, but I am certainly no authority on this subject!

Chapter 16

Evelyn Meets Paul

Paul and Evelyn, Dec 2010

After finding out about Ed's rebirth, I began to feel very deserted, which was probably a healthy development. I knew there was no use in trying to contact him. I was finally beginning to reach the end of settling his trust, and I was devoting more energy into developing some relationships here in the Bandon community. Ed had passed away not long after our move from California, and we knew very few people when we moved to Oregon. My only goal was developing some close relationships with a few female friends. I had absolutely no interest in dating or ever getting married again. Three marriages were more than I had ever anticipated in this lifetime, and a fourth was definitely not anything I had ever considered. However, fate, it seemed, acts in strange, unexpected ways!

On September 19, 2010, I attended church at Unity of Bandon just as I had done on a fairly regular basis since Ed passed over. I was somewhat late so hurriedly headed for my usual seat next to the aisle on the left. However, a man had already taken my seat, so I stepped over him and sat down next to him. We never looked at each other during the service, but I did note that he had a cane, so it was my thought toward the end that I would introduce myself as a friendly member of the church. It turned out that he had a cane because he was recovering from knee surgery. He apparently knew very few people at Unity. After discovering that he had met my late husband Ed at the Senior Center, I suggested we have lunch together. I am still rather amazed that I had enough nerve to do that; my guides must have been sending me some strong messages! Paul and I totally enjoyed a prolonged lunch at one of Bandon's best restaurants overlooking the Pacific Ocean. Our discussion was mainly about wanting to have a good companion to dine with occasionally, exchanging information about ourselves, and both stating very definitely that we were not interested in getting married again (Paul had recently gone through a very stressful divorce.)

We had driven to the restaurant in our separate cars, and as we were parting, Paul gave me a big hug, which startled me. I had mentioned during our lunch that I wanted to go to an excellent restaurant that was soon closing. Would he be interested in going with me? I later learned that Paul has a hearing problem and really didn't understand what I was saying about the restaurant, so there was no decision about meeting again.

After not hearing anything from Paul for three days, I decided to send him an e-mail, apologizing for being so forward and that maybe going to Rosie's Bistro was not a very good idea. He sent the following reply:

> Thank you so very much for taking the seat next to me in church Sunday, and for the open manner in which you spoke with me. Thank you too for your kind words about our conversation over lunch. Do you suppose "a little bird" opened the way for each of us? I must also admit that we were rather surprised about how well those moments went, and I too want that, or something just as real to happen again soon.
>
> I had no hesitation in accepting the opportunity to talk with someone "without an agenda," with intelligence, competence and self-assurance. At first I almost stumbled to reply to your greeting, but immediately got on the same line with you, and accepted your request for "company;" I could easily have made the same request of you. However, since that was my first time back to Unity in more than two

years, I wanted to ensure that I had heard you correctly.

In retrospect, I find nothing but respect that you would honestly want me to go for lunch, having only met each other seconds before. Again, I thank you.

Please, let's go together to Rose's, any night you would like to go. My calendar is clean as a whistle, and needs some attention.

I too will be very careful the rest of my life with any involvement in a relationship that neither of us would like, and which does not acknowledge our personal desire for 'open space,' without crowding.

Are we experiencing a degree of serendipity?

Paul

I should explain that when I knew Carroll and Wally there was no such thing as e-mail to my knowledge, and when I first met Ed neither he nor I were into e-mails. Beginning a relationship electronically was a whole new experience for me. Paul writes beautifully, so while I shall eliminate part of his messages, I feel that he can express the beauty of our relationship far better than I. I have thought about publishing a book composed of all of his e-mails, which are mostly beautiful love letters to me, and a tribute to Nature. His descriptions of the views from his home are sheer poetry. Any of you who would like to take these letters as romantic inspiration, feel free to copy! Keep in mind that when we met I was 78 and Paul was 80.

We both feel as if we are with the love of our life, and are so very grateful to have finally met again. Prior to our meeting Paul had very little knowledge about reincarnation, but readily agreed that we must have known each other before, because of our instant attraction to each other. It took a very long time to get any information from Athor about our soul relationship, so I was going strictly by my own intuition and feelings, even though, as you will later see, this was an extremely unlikely match due to our backgrounds.

I had responded to Paul's first e-mail by stating that I wondered what I was doing?? Paul's response:

Me too, what am I doing? However, I want to say clearly that I am very comfortable with all our conversation, expressed desires for the type and degree of company, and the ease with which we have moved to this moment. I feel honored to have shared our Sunday experience and look forward to other shared times as opportunity presents itself.

(Later the same day) One place I want to take you is to Hilltop Restaurant in North Bend. It's not overly fancy, and a good menu of excellent food is available. That is one of my favorite places to eat in Coos County. We'll talk later about a time to go.

Please feel free to "ramble on" any time, (in reference to my e-mail apology for rambling on) that gives me license to do the same. I feel very good about our conversing in person or email, and one day/night we'll talk by phone. I really like the sound of your voice, and am anxious to hear more of it.

It seems to me already that we will not have a shortage of things to talk about. I can think now of at least a dozen areas I want to explore with you, and not just housekeeping and food. I feel I can speak freely, and look forward to doing so.

Regards, Paul

(Two hours later) Saturday evening at 5:15 cannot come quickly enough. You fascinate me to no end; I indeed want to know much more about you. I am anxious for some philosophical discussion, something I have had few people to talk with in a long, long time. Although my major in college was Psychology, and studies for a second BA were in Philosophy and Religion, I actually learned little more than to spell each word. Conservative religion was consuming me at the time. No more!
Enjoy the rest of the evening.
Paul

(One day later) I'll comment on your last message first. I sincerely request that you scold me for my non-stop jabbering, but 'I jes can't help it'. You have whetted my interest to the boiling point. Now see what you have done?

I concur entirely with your opinion. You speak my case exactly when you state that 'life' in the REAL WORLD is THE learning medium. Experiencing life in all its complexities, problems and successes is the arena from which I have come to be who I am, what I know (or think I know,) what I achieve to be, and shall continue to be my 'workshop.' I wasn't brave enough to speak up to my professors as you apparently were, although I knew deep inside that real life experiences would be not only my real teacher, but where I sharpened my teeth and ground my ax for future learning and growth to fuller stature.

(Later that night) Is it OK if both of us feel like teenagers? I vote "yea." Let's just "go with the flow" and see what happens. I feel complete trust in you and sense that you have some comfort with how we have proceeded to know each other better (just lots of e-mails after our long lunch, actually!) I want you to know that I do not assume any particular outcome, but am persuaded that I want to know all about you and you to know all about me. I have no hidden agenda and no tricks up my sleeve. I want to earn your acceptance as a friend and as a comrade in intelligent conversation. I invite any and all questions, and will respond honestly and completely.

(Later that night) Hey, it appears that I am two years older than you. I was born January 16, 1930, a Capricorn. I graduated in '47 at the age of 17. There were 117 in my graduating class, and although I was class president, I didn't set the world on fire with high grades. We'll talk more about this, eh?

It was finally Saturday night, and time for our much anticipated dinner together. The food was excellent, although ridiculously expensive; great wine and stimulating conversation. I continued to be extremely nervous, and apparently Paul was too. He again hugged me before he went home, but was a perfect gentleman, saying repeatedly, that he didn't want to 'mess this up.' We agreed to meet at church again the next day, followed up by lunch afterward.

Paul had mentioned that his home was on a cliff overlooking the Coquille River and the ocean. I decided that it

171

was time to pay him a visit after I did his numerology, which revealed several master numbers in his profile.

He had gone up to Salem, Oregon to check on his knee which was still giving him problems. I discovered that I would really miss him if anything happened to him. That is a long trip for someone to drive with a bum knee, so I was greatly relieved when he had returned home safely. When I walked in the door I gave HIM a big hug and a kiss. Numerology and metaphysics in general were foreign to him, but he listened politely to my explanation of his numbers and seemed to find it interesting.

I had brought a DVD from Netflix which I thought might be a good film to watch, since it was about the afterlife. So, we sat on the sofa, holding hands. The movie became dumber and dumber, we were both bored, and I was beginning to have feelings that I had not felt in a very long time. All Paul was doing was rubbing his fingers over my hands, but I was really turned on! Since I had met him, I had become aware of a very uncomfortable vibration in my body, something I had only experienced one other time when I met a man whom I had known Off-Earth. It was not really a sexual feeling at the beginning, but when he started touching me it was like electricity. I finally turned around on the sofa and let him just hold me. It was an amazing feeling!

My visit that afternoon was followed by another e-mail:

> My, how I enjoyed your visit this afternoon; I especially appreciate your reading of my numbers. How fascinating, and yet I can honestly say that I am not surprised that you and I have so many numbers alike.

And…..oooohhh, how nice to hold you in my arms and feel you lying against my chest. I love so very much to just be close to you, and holding you is such an intimate way of saying …I really like you.

I must close and go read before I start another marathon of writing, this time about you, as well as to you. I look forward to all the coming minutes, hours and other units of time that we may be together. Fondly (this is intended to sound personal, very personal,)
Paul

In addition to doing Paul's numerology, I gave him a copy of my book, which was another big test of whether we could have a relationship.

E-mail 11 days after we had met:

G'day to you, Sweet Lady. I'm finding it hard to change thinking subjects from you, you and me …us. And it's all music in my mind and body. If I wasn't so awfully clumsy I'd be dancing throughout the house and outside. I'd find it impossible to ever lose you as my friend, as well as "more." Serendipity would put a strangle hold on me for doing or saying anything that might jeopardize our relationship. "S" brought us together, "S' is with us, and I'm willing to go wherever "S" leads us. This is "puddin proof" that Something, Someone, or an assistant to one of those entities is operating full force. Some of my analogies may be rather dumb or infantile, but I'm sure you can decipher what I am saying.

I slept very well after I finally put down your book around 3:30 AM. Your book cannot be read in a week, in fact it will not be fully read until I can return, perhaps several times to incidents/events you wrote about that need much concentration. After all, I am a babe in the field of reality (yes, I have already decided it IS reality,) so I will need your patience and help. OK? I am bowled over with excitement at the "happenings" we have experienced in such a short time. And I tell you for sure, I ain't putting on any brakes. However, I want to be soft, kind and loving to you in a manner that you will know without question that I sincerely care for you. Our next togetherness will not come too soon for me, and I am sensing that your desires are mutual. My lands, I have been smitten!

Hugs and kisses, Paul

It was right around this time that Paul finally called me on the telephone and said that it was difficult to be the first one to say "I love you", but he was going to say it. I told him that I thought I loved him, but still was not really sure, since that seemed like such a commitment.

I had learned that Paul had a very difficult childhood. His father had left the family when Paul was two years old, subsequently remarrying. He gave very little support to the family; Paul's mother worked long hours to support her two children, so there was very little affectionate mothering. Paul married a girl he met in college when he was 19, and became a father of a son and daughter at a very young age. His mother and all of his relatives were extremely religious; Methodist on his mother's side, and Nazarene on his father's side. He was forced to go to church twice a week, starting when he was a toddler. During the Korean War Paul joined the Air Force as an Airman, and was promoted to Staff Sergeant during his four year stint. What really amazed me, however, was his telling me that he had been a Methodist minister, and then a Nazarene minister, for 19 years! He became quite disillusioned with religion and would have nothing to do with it until he had attended Unity Church two years before we met. Then he decided to come back to church just for something to do that fateful day in September. This should have totally alarmed me, with my strong metaphysical beliefs, but instead I found it rather intriguing. Paul had been married for 22 years to his first wife and was then divorced; his second marriage lasted 31 years. He met his third wife over the Internet, and it seemingly was a disaster from the beginning. In his mind he had failed two marriages, and was determined to make this last one work, so he stuck with it much longer than he should have.

As a therapist, all of this rather alarmed me. If a client were talking to me about a prospective relationship, I could not have encouraged such a union. I expressed all of these concerns to Paul, and he understood why I would have doubts about progressing with a serious relationship. I had no doubt about how I felt about Paul, but getting involved with him did not seem to be a very rational thing to do. I was totally convinced that we had a past life relationship, and I felt that it began Off-Earth because of the strange vibrations in my body that I was experiencing when we first met. Paul replied to my comments about the vibrations I was feeling:

Sweetheart Ev,

I like the sound of that, and hope you do too. Every contact I have with you, phone, and e-mail and in person, I feel closer and closer to you; and when I have held you I feel I want to pull you into my being. I am anxious to hear more about the other time when your cells started vibrating. I tell you for certain that I have had no one make me feel that our physical touching was so right in such a short time after meeting. I get so very, very horny when you are in my arms. I agree with you that 'we' are more than a case of nerves. You turn me on when I'm reading your emails, when we talk on the phone and (Wowee...) when we touch.

Thank you for asking me to call you each night before we try to go to sleep. It is apparent that both of us want the same soul touch before we turn out the light. Saturday will surely be a good day for us, whatever the weather and whatever we do. Between now and then I'll develop a menu of choices that I believe both of us will enjoy. I can hardly wait to see and hold you again.

Until tonight,

Hugs and Kisses, Paul

I was still attempting to get an Athor reading about our soul relationship, with little success due to her health problems. I have a good friend who does astrology, so I decided to check this out. This was a confirmation of why we are so attracted to each other. Paul is a Capricorn and I am an Aquarian, but they are both January birthdates. Both of our moons are Leo, and both of our ascendants are Sagittarius, both fire signs. Very likely, if we had met earlier in life we would have had a stormy relationship; but of course, we would have been so far apart in our belief systems that we would not have been interested in each other. At this point in his life, Paul was ready for a huge shift in his thinking. Who knows? This may be due to the seemingly global shift into higher consciousness. At any rate, I have definitely found a physical and spiritual partner, as well as a best friend; something I have never experienced before in any relationship. So those of you who feel you have never met the "right" one, don't give up hope! It might happen when you least expect it.

Chapter 17

Paul's Near-Death Experience

Paul, Dec 2010

Once again I was involved with a man who had a near death experience. As with Ed, I seriously doubt I would have been attracted to Paul before this happened. I have asked him to give the story in his own words:

June 23, 2009 I underwent surgery at Oregon Health and Science University in Portland Oregon for repair of two ribs; they had failed to form a union following a fall during the night of September 23, 2008. Mine was one of less than fifty experimental surgeries to repair rib fractures in a specially funded Program sponsored by the Federal Government. My daughter Lynda came from San Diego to be with me all of my stay in the hospital, and to drive me back home upon discharge. My best friend, Bob, also came frequently to see me and try his best to lift my spirits.

Following surgery, I began recuperation in a post-surgical ICU. During that period I remember (real or imagined) that one or more nurses, including the nurse-researcher managing the Program, were almost constantly attentive to ensure that my pain was adequately controlled and all other needs were met. I remember having little or no pain.

Later (one or two days?), I was moved to another "ICU" that I perceived was in another wing of the hospital. It was accessed only by being rolled on a gurney across two or three planks spanning the gap between the two parts of the building. Immediately upon being rolled out of the first "ICU' everything was darkening, finally becoming black, and the hallway was illuminated only by two single light bulbs suspended from the ceiling.

Upon entering the second "ICU" everything remained pitch dark, with only one light bulb suspended from the ceiling. The room was perhaps as large as a basketball court. I heard lots of moans and cries of pain from people all over that room, none of whom I could actually see, and was unaware if any of them were receiving care.

Pain in the surgical area of my back grew increasingly severe, and the one attending nurse did not bring me meds for pain control, other than aspirin. I felt desperately alone, without access to anyone who could/would (?) help me find relief from my pain and my predicament. I kept calling out for the nurse to bring relief. During the few times she came to my bedside I could barely make out her image in the darkness.

The pain continued to get unbearably severe, and I started having cramping chest pains. When I told the nurse, she issued a 'code call.' Almost immediately several doctors, nurses and firemen came, picked me up from the bed, and lay me on the floor in the dimly lighted hallway. A large burly firemen "took control" of everything, with different persons checking my BP, pulse, etc. The fireman opened my mouth with his large thumb, and placed a nitroglycerin tablet under my tongue. A lady physician knelt beside me, and asked more than once, "...if your heart stops beating and you cease breathing, do you want us to attempt resuscitation by compressions or other means..." I responded slowly, but certainly, that I wanted no attempt to resuscitate me. I felt very faint, and believed that I was dying, or would be soon. Each time I repeated my decision I felt I was slowly losing consciousness, and the room began to get darker and darker.

After what seemed (?) an hour or more, the large fireman stood erect and announced '...this man is

NOT having a heart attack!', and started walking away. At that announcement I felt more hopeless than ever; again, I was quickly losing consciousness. I felt absolutely hopeless. The medical staff who had gathered put me back into my bed and drifted away. I was back in that awful darkness. The nurse must have given me a narcotic, because the next thing I remember I was being rolled out of that darkness, across the planks spanning the gap between buildings, down a long hallway, around several corners, and finally placed in the only bed in another 'ICU."

While in this second "ICU" my pain was only partially controlled, but nothing was given or done to alleviate the desperate feeling of aloneness. I felt that this "ICU" was my "final resting place" before I would lose consciousness for good. I believed the only nurse available to tend me was secretly watching from a distance for any "changes" to take place. I also believed my daughter had deserted me, and was intentionally staying away from the hospital. (I found out later that she had been to see me every day, and visited for long periods.) After much complaining of pain and desertion, my surgeon came to see me. Upon relating my feelings and concerns to him he said I would be transferred to yet another "ICU."

Soon after my surgeon left I was moved to the new room; I was the only patient, although there were two beds in the room. As soon as I was settled in bed, a young black "waitress" appeared with a tray of goodies held high on one hand; she said I could choose any treat. She also offered to bring me "anything else" I wished. I believed that her offer could possibly include sex, although no actions on her part confirmed that offer, nor did I have any interest in pursuing it.

The strangeness of being in a really delightful, airy, appealing room, and having a lovely young lady "serve" me with goodies, led me to believe that I had actually left the prior human existence of pain and other discomfort, and was in reality (?) in another existence. My major discomfort at this time was the sound of voices from outside my door, and the fleeting sight of persons walking by. I believed plans were being made for me that would not be revealed to me ...good or bad, with emphasis on the latter.

It was only after two or three days that I began to realize that I was indeed recuperating from surgery and that everything now happening to or for me was routine medical care. My paranoia diminished significantly, and I sincerely believed that I was getting good medical care. My pain was largely controlled by narcotics, and I was otherwise comfortable.

My best friend Bob and my daughter Lynda visited me regularly. As each visited, I began to understand what had actually happened to me. I learned where I had been cared for, especially during the "dark" periods, and that no one was out to "get me;" no one had ever been "after me."

The first few times Bob visited me in this last room, he emphatically stated that I MUST get over this "nonsensical funk," and know that I was loved without measure by all my close friends. THAT (my capitals for emphasis) was the beginning of a new outlook on life for me. My prior tendency had been to quickly blame others for little or nothing; then my generous trust of others was a significant change in my persona. To me, I have become a much more complete person in every way. Life for me is so very meaningful, and I intend to continue this road of personal endeavor.

This is not the typical near-death experience. However, Paul told me this story shortly after we met. It apparently left a deep impression in his psyche, and when I heard it I began to wonder just what really happened to him. I recall asking Paul the kind of questions I would ask a person who thought he/she might have been a "walk-in," since these experiments often happened during a near death experience.

Prior to this episode in the hospital he had been deeply depressed, having gone through three divorces - all of them very traumatic experiences; again a circumstance often preceding a "walk-in" experiment. However, Paul was very clear that he did not feel that he was a "different" person as in the case of a person who is a "walk-in". But he did sense a definite change in his way of thinking and acting toward others. In a sense, his experience was similar to people who have gone into what they described as a kind of hell, when they almost died, then the very last memories were of being in a place somewhat like a heaven when the nurse came in and said he could have anything he wanted.

As time went on and my relationship with Paul continued to deepen, I wanted more specifics about our past life relationship, but Athor's health continued to prevent her from feeling she could give accurate readings. It was not until December 30, 2010 that she finally agreed to do another reading for me.

One of the main items I addressed was about his near-death experience. Some of this is paraphrased to give more clarity for the reader.

Athor: There appears to be either a choking or loss of air situation. As he is losing consciousness he is traveling through the dimensions without accessing or processing any particular dimension, per se. We are trying to see where he ended up or why that occurred. There is some kind of past life experience in which he was praying or meditating very strongly, and he had an out of body experience in that cycle in which he experienced a great blinding light. There was something in the psyche he felt in that life was not completed. It was like the soul longed for more. It wanted to see or feel more because it felt its experience was cut off in that life. In this life, that was one of the things that triggered this experience of the so-called near death experience.

There appears in this life to have been a greater sense of satisfaction than in that other lifetime, but something was still missing. The near death experience was karmically necessary. It absolved a lot of karma basically for the Paul being. A lot of mistaken beliefs and misunderstandings that the being had carried were wiped clean due to this experience, so it was necessary on many levels.

Evelyn: During this "out of body" trip, did part of his higher-self come in? Did he become more of an enlightened being?

Athor: In the sense that certain energies had been removed which were blocking some vision and understanding, yes, in that sense. There are many levels in the dimensions, and apparently he was traveling through the lower astral planes which can be like our vision of hell.

I began to wonder what Paul's hospital records would show. When Paul received them, he found voluminous documentation of the results of all his blood tests which didn't mean much to us, but they also indicated he was in the ICU several times and he apparently did have a heart attack plus a collapsed lung. All of this was after the initial surgery. The records did not give the names of the pain medications administered which as we know can create hallucinations. Whatever happened, Paul THOUGHT he had died.

P.M.H. Atwater recently completed a large treatise on her research entitled *Near-Death Experiences: The Rest of the Story*. She discusses many different types of near death experiences that are not the traditional "going into the Light" type. Among those experiences some, like Paul, perceive a reality which is distressing or Hellish as if a confrontation with distortions in one's own attitudes and beliefs. These often result in a healing of the psyche. Considering the misunderstandings due his religious beliefs that Athor discusses, this would seem to be an appropriate near-death experience for Paul.

Chapter 18

Past Life Relationships of Evelyn and Paul

Evelyn and Paul's Marriage January 20, 2011

When I asked Aki/Athor to do a past life reading for Paul and myself, my chief interest was in finding out if we indeed had known each other before incarnating here on Earth. As discussed previously, I was experiencing a strange, uncomfortable vibration in my body when we first met, and from all I have learned about soul relationships this seemed to indicate existences together Off-Earth. However, I wanted validation of this from another source. In previous readings from Athor I knew that she needed to be instructed to go Off-Earth, because in order to do so, she needed to adjust her energy to a different level. She is seemingly now channeling the Athor energy through Aki which is more difficult for her since she is going through a human channel. All of the other Off-Earth readings were conducted when Athor was still in a human body.

Evelyn: I would like to know if Paul and I had any Off-Earth experiences together. (We then went through the usual procedure of stating both full names.)
Athor: This is not so easy. I am searching. The pictures are not coming readily. There are many subconscious blockages from past lives that have been very traumatic for that being. He is carrying a great deal of scaring. I am seeing that he had some scientific type of job or position. It looks like he was on some kind of committee sort like the Council of Sirius, but maybe not quite like that; but it was some governing body. In that capacity he had to lay down some rules or pass some rules and whatever he did in that aspect had to do with some scientific work As a consequence, because of this scientific work, something went wrong. Although he wasn't like a mad scientist in the films, so to speak, he felt extremely guilty, extremely responsible. And that set the stage for him to get a lot of scaring in his psyche, which led to many traumatic life cycles on Earth.

You are not showing up yet. Let me see if I can find you here. You were another member on that committee, council or whatever it was, but you had a secondary role. It wasn't like everybody there had equal billing, so to speak. You were all members of the same council, but you all had different positions and jobs. So yours was not quite at the level of decision making that he had to make. You did not have a ruling voice there; whereas, he did more so. It is not to say that there was dissension. You might have been his wife or someone of that nature, but it is not coming clearly at all. You had some influence on him besides being on that council as a member of the governing body. It was not a strong Earth-bound, Earth-based cord between the two of you. In that existence you were not together very long for some reason.

Evelyn: How many people were on the council?

Athor: Maybe fifteen or twenty.

Evelyn: What star system was this connected to?

Athor: I don't know if they have named that - something like Raded or Radei. It is not certain if it is in this Milky Way galaxy.

Evelyn: Were we in physical bodies in that existence?

Athor: The physical form was not exactly the same as on Earth. There was more of an air-type quality; it wasn't oxygen like we know, but the bodies were composed of more air-like qualities than human bodies that are carbon based. This was a different structure. It could be called physical, but not in terms of how it is on Earth. It was more of an air element to the vehicles.

Evelyn: Were there any other Off-Earth existences together?

Athor: Yes, but not even semi-solid forms. There seems to be more connected with this being in the inter and intra dimensional space. This is not to say that these were the so-called in-between space, between physical life and physical death, wherein the spirit goes into certain astral realms. These are not the same astral realms. They are different. These were created for experiencing life in a different sense. I hear that there were many encounters in these special realms wherein you two interacted, but to try to explain this in Earth base terms is impossible. There is simply no similarity.

Evelyn: Okay, let's go to Earth lives together.

Athor: It zeros in on two people. They are on a beach around a lake, and they are sitting on a blanket and discussing life, I hear. They appear to be of the opposite sex. Dusk is coming, so they get up and end up in a house; this house looks like a European house. It has a chimney, and there is smoke coming out. Evidently it was starting to get cool at dusk, and somebody must have been at home to build a fire. It appears that the house is fairly large, and there are some other people there, so these two are not the only occupants of the house. They go into one of the rooms.

They appear to be fairly young, maybe in the early to mid-twenties. And they continue their discussion. There is some romantic interlude. (Athor states that she usually does not see sexual encounters, as has been the case in the hundreds of readings she did for my clients.) I hear that he was not ready to settle down in that lifetime. I don't see any violent disagreement, but there seems to be a lack of consensus in that scene because the man is afraid in that life. He is afraid of commitment, and he wants to be free in that life.

There is something hanging over him at that point. It is like a trap. This is hard to get because he has all those blocks he is still carrying, that energy. When I ask what specifically needs to be seen about that life, I hear the word obsession. I am looking into the energy; it looks like he had an obsessive nature in that life and that was the barrier that you couldn't get through. Even though there was love there, and a limited relationship because of his obsessive nature, for you the relationship was less than satisfactory. You couldn't meet on the same level in order to have a long lasting relationship in that life. The relationship didn't last long because he was on another track. This is what needs to be repaired and made whole, basically. This is why you have come together. As you have had all these other cycles and other experiences, he is finally ready to fully let go of these karmic scars that were involved in your relationship with him, and his relationships to others.

This is a positive thing; rather than karma where two people are brought together because they still have negative things to complete, to still fight out at times. It is not like that. This is different. And there are other lives you have had.

This is a very involved story, but basically Paul was a leader of a group of soldiers who came to a small town to hunt down some of the men in the town who were their enemies. The small group of men from the village was no match for the large group of soldiers; therefore, they were all killed except a young boy who was held as a hostage. The leader of the soldiers apparently is somehow related to this young boy and did not want to see him die, but he wanted to teach him a lesson regarding his joining up with the men who were killed.

The young boy (Evelyn) was hung, but not by his neck. He hangs from a tree to let him know this is what we do with unruly children. The boy is dangling there, but not very high because he was hung in such a way that when somebody finds him, or if he finally does fall, he won't have serious injuries. In the meantime he would be out of the way long enough for the soldiers to meet back with the main brigade.

Some people from the village indeed did find him and cut him down. As the young man grew up he never forgot the man who was the leader of the soldiers. He felt gratitude that he wasn't killed, because the man could have killed him. Had he been so inclined he could also have tortured him. Instead, he treated him like a young upstart type of thing, because Athor later determined, that the man (Paul) was in fact the uncle of the boy (Evelyn.)

I was glad to receive confirmation that Paul and I have been together many times, although by then we were so much in love that it would not have made any difference what Athor came up with in a reading. I continue to be very interested in research on the soul, Off-Earth lives, etc., so I was mainly interested in the reading from the viewpoint of research. Since there were repeated references to Paul's many traumatic lives, we followed this up with a reading strictly about the journey of Paul's soul. But before going into that in the next chapter I want to include what I feel is one of the main purposes of our meeting again. I asked Athor could she see anything that Paul and I can do together to help Planet Earth at this crucial time of its history?

Athor: Yes. First of all, you can get together physically or on the phone on a daily basis and do the following visualization. Sit opposite each other if you are together physically, far enough away to imagine that the circle that you are sitting in is a ring of Light. This is a white light with rainbow colors swirling around. Place the Planet Earth in the center of this circle, and ask for all the Beings of Light who wish to assist in bringing peace, harmony, good will and balance to this Planet to do so. Invoke the highest Beings of Light to protect the Earth and all of its inhabitants.

If you can get other people together, that would make it even better. If you could get a group together, the energy would increase exponentially. It is saying that if there were such groups in every city and town doing this once a day, the impact would be enormous.

Paul and I have started a "Light Group" that meets once a month at his home. We have a format that includes this meditation, plus various other appropriate meditations to assist the Earth. Every day we do the brief version as stated above, followed by a blessing of the food we eat, something that neither of us has done for many years. It sets a positive tone for the day and I urge all of my readers to memorize this brief meditation and add to it as you desire. This could be done alone or with as many people as you wish. It is POWERFUL!!

Chapter 19

A Brief Review of Paul's Life

Rev Paul Mounts 1955.

In order to understand the relevance of the Athor reading for Paul, I feel it is helpful to know more about this lifetime here on Earth.

Paul was born in Marion, Kentucky in January, 1930, right at the beginning of the great depression. His father deserted the family when Paul was two years old; he lived with his older brother and mother at almost the poverty level due to the fact his father never contributed financially to the family. He was ill quite a lot as a child. He also had to stay at home at times to do cleaning, while his brother was allowed to go be with his friends. Sometimes he helped with the cooking. His mother worked outside the home very long hours, and was usually too exhausted to do much mothering. Paul's older brother was very athletic and quite social, and was away from home much of the time, and not interested in having his younger brother tag along.

Paul's mother was a member of the very conservative Southern Methodist Church. This involved attending church twice on Sunday and Wednesday night prayer meeting. Paul did not like it, but was always required to attend from a very young age. When I did a regression with Paul, he went back to the time when he was about two. He had a clear memory of having to sit on a stool in a Bible class for adults because he cried or misbehaved with the other children who were attending in other classrooms. The mantra in his house was, "don't smoke, don't drink, don't dance, don't, don't, don't!" With this background, it is amazing to me that later in high school he was president of his senior class, a cheerleader, and obviously quite popular.

With much encouragement from the church and his family he entered the Methodist ministry at age 17 with a license to preach. During this time he attended Asbury College in Wilmore, Kentucky. Lack of finances made it impossible to continue at Asbury until graduation. As he told me in one of our early e-mails, he made one of the biggest mistakes of his life when he decided to marry at age 19. After his marriage, he was assigned as minister of the (northern) Methodist

Church in Grandview, Indiana. After eight months in this assignment, he resigned and joined the Nazarene Church where he was assigned during the next sixteen years to various locations around the country.

In 1954 Paul joined the U.S. Air Force for four years, going from Airman to Staff Sergeant. This enabled him to return to school through the GI bill; he earned a B.A. in psychology, and had a year of additional studies in philosophy and religion.

Finally, in 1966, having become very disillusioned with the religious hierarchy and politics of the church, he gave up the traditional religious life in the church and moved on to a totally different career in social work.

His professional career of 32 years of government services ended with his retirement from the State of Oregon where he was a Medicaid Program Manager, and a Medical Auditor. This kind of background seems to have been a continuation of many lives in the religious domain.

Chapter 20

Paul's Past Lives

Stormy Pacific

When we were finally able to get another Athor reading for Paul in December 2010, his questions all revolved around his most difficult relationships. The first reading had just covered the highlights of our past lives together. As stated earlier, Paul was first married at age 19, and it was never a very compatible relationship. However, he was a minister and tried to stick it out because of his children - a son and a daughter whom he dearly loved. When he finally left the ministry, he realized that he was in an unhappy relationship. So after 22 years of marriage, he decided that was enough, and he left that home with little more than the clothes on his back. I have never heard him say anything really negative about his first wife; therefore, he did not ask Athor about her. By this time in the marriage they had widely different interests which were irreconcilable.

His second marriage began with both Pat and Paul being very happy. Their relationship was quite positive for many years, according to Paul. When she had extensive surgery in 1980, it seems something happened to her mentally and emotionally while in the hospital. Many people die in hospitals, so I have speculated that she perhaps may have been possessed by an earthbound spirit. He didn't understand why she seemed to become a different person when she returned home from the hospital. We had discussed this situation many times; it totally has puzzled Paul as to how she could become so different. Therefore, his first question to Athor was about Pat.

Evelyn: What is the past life relationship between (gives full names) of Paul and Pat?
Athor: We have a scene where it is quite chaotic. There are many people in this tent type thing. It is a fairly large room and they are all having an argument. There are 20-30 people arguing about something. Someone gets up at the head of the room and yells for order and wants to be heard. We see that this person is trying to obviously calm everyone down with what he is saying. There is a lot of grumbling and people are not necessarily in agreement with what this man is saying. He is telling them to bide their time and wait before they jump to any further conclusions, so the people go home. There is one couple, a man and a woman who

are going home. This is a rural area and they are going home to their ranch house. This appears to be the time period when there was the westward movement in the United States.

After reaching home, the man and woman are discussing whatever had gone on at the meeting, and they are not in agreement with each other. The man decides he is going to do something about the situation that was discussed at the meeting. The woman is frantically trying to get him to stop, but he won't stop. He goes on out and gets shot. He is not killed, but is severely wounded to the point where he cannot function, and appears to be paralyzed and cannot walk. He can speak, but he can't walk. A group of men bring him back to the ranch house.

The man was the present day gentleman Paul, and the woman was the present day Pat. In that lifetime they had three children. She wanted him to help raise those three children and he couldn't really do it. There is a nine year old boy, a two year old and five year old. Since they are all quite young, the nine year boy has a lot of responsibility because of this. The other two are kind of left on their own because the wife cannot keep up with the work. She has to tend to her invalid husband, take care of the ranch and the children, and she just cannot do it. It is seen that one of the two children wanders off and falls into a large pit and was severely injured, dying in that lifetime.

Now there are only two children, so the wife gets an uncle to come and help out. He comes over and does as many of the ranch chores as possible, but she still cannot keep up with the work. It is seen at the end of that life cycle she falls into a deep, deep depression. She couldn't maintain what was required. Having lost the one child, the older child became kind of wild, and he does not help out because he has such a wild streak. The wife becomes non-functional within a period of three to five years from the time the husband was injured.

It is seen that the same reaction was precipitated by a poor choice in this lifetime (Pat had decided to have both breasts removed, even though there was no clear evidence that she had cancer. During the surgery she also had breast implants, which did not go well, with one breast being larger than the other,) plus a large chain of karmic circumstances. She had ended that last life in a deep depression, and the surgery appears to have triggered her psychotic condition in this lifetime.

There were subconscious memories of the overwhelming problems in that Western lifetime with Paul. Obviously there must have been other positive lifetimes, since they had a good relationship for many years; but we are looking at the one that needs to be resolved as far as the karmic connection goes.

Evelyn: Pat and Paul were married for 31 years but have had no contact for seven years. Is she still alive?

Athor: Yes she is, but she is still not doing all that well. There is darkness. She seems to be in a deeply crazed condition. There are energies within the being which obviously need to be resolved, but will not be resolved in this lifetime; this is not to say that the energies between these two beings are waiting for future karmic resolution. It is seen that this being here today

(Paul) has done much to dissolve and resolve the karmic bonds. The two came together to continue on in a sense where they left off in the previous life. They did not have a so-called bad relationship in that prior life. It was simply when he got shot and things went downhill that she mentally broke down, and eventually ended that life cycle deeply depressed.

Evelyn: What happened to Paul in that lifetime if he was paralyzed and she died? How did that life end?

Athor: There were some family members who came and moved in. They basically took over the ranch, and brought their children so there was a big, big family there. They cared for him as much as they could. He lived another two, maybe three years and then he died. He did not have a long life cycle, being about 32 when he died in that life.

Evelyn: About what dates are we talking about?

Athor: It is seen that he passed on in 1840 or 1841.

Evelyn: You said this was in the American West. Can you be more specific than that?

Athor: Utah.

Evelyn: Could this possibly have been a Mormon family?

Athor: Yes, it is quite possible, since there are such a large number of people in this family unit. It seems odd that he could not get more assistance while he was alive. One moment; we wish to look further at that life. Well, they were his relatives that came to care for him when she passed on. They came and moved in. There were lots of circumstances that prevented them from coming and moving in at an earlier time. They were busy with other events in their lives, up until the time his wife died. Then events opened up so they could come and move in.

Evelyn: Would you ask specifically if these relatives were Mormons?

Athor: It appears so. This being Paul was either related or connected to Brigham Young.

I wish we had pursued this line of questioning to get more facts, but I was so shocked that I just dropped it. Paul had a very difficult relationship with his father, who had deserted the family when Paul was two years old; therefore, his second priority regarding a past life was with his father. As usual, I gave the full names of Paul and then his father.

Athor: There appears to be at least one man with a muff-like armor on, and a helmet with a spike on top. He is sitting on a horse overlooking a valley. He appears to be scouting, checking out something, because further back there are a number of troops. He is overlooking this valley, and there is smoke coming out from cottages from wood fires as they try to stay warm. He seems to go down this mountain by himself, very slowly on the horse. Perhaps he is trying to get a closer look.

Whoever this man is, the energy is like the story of Don Quixote, who used to chase windmills. He is slowly riding down, and then comes to the bottom of the mountain where there is an encampment of soldiers. He rides in there, and goes to one tent-type structure and gets off the horse. He appears to be tired. That is why it is taking so long. He goes into this tent and collapses from fatigue, it appears. Some other soldiers, who do not have their armor on, came into the tent.

They come in and take the armor off of him. It is seen that he was wounded, and that is why he collapsed. There appears to be an injury in the left groin from a lance or sword. The bleeding has almost coagulated by then, but the injury is quite painful, and he has lost a lot of blood in the stomach. The other soldiers basically cauterize the wound to keep it from opening up again. It is not seen that there is any stitching done at that time or place.

He falls into what we hear is a troubled sleep, and has all these nightmares of battle scenes. In this nightmare he is having, there is one soldier that stands out, and it is the man that gave him the injury. In the nightmare the man keeps coming back, threatening him, which is debilitating to him. There seems to be a family relationship in that past life between the two particular individuals. In that life they were brothers, but then they parted ways partly because of different belief systems, different political persuasions, and it is seen that they ended up in two different armies because of this. He was injured in this recent battle by this brother.

Besides having the nightmares he has a fever, because it has been several days since he sustained the injury and an infection has arisen in him. This is another reason that he is having this nightmare, and he is beginning to hallucinate in his waking state about this other man coming to kill him. The fever has caused these delusions; his men had tried unsuccessfully is get his fever down. It is seen that he lingers for a few days, and then dies. *(Athor asks for the names to be stated again.)* Paul is the being in that lifetime that died from his injuries; his father in this lifetime was the one from the other army.

Evelyn: Give me an approximate time period.

Athor: The late fifteen hundreds, or fourteen hundreds; I hear 1453.

Evelyn: What country?

Athor: The area called Prussia.

Evelyn: Does religion play a major role between Paul and his father? His father was almost fanatically religious.

Athor: We will need to look at the father Being independently. (Long pause) There is a scene where there appears to be some type of monastery in an eastern land. Inside the walls of this monastic order, the beings do great penance. There is self-flagellation, with whips and things like that, and then they also do this to each other. There is much fasting and great penance. I also see a scene of torture in the medieval age, and another lifetime when the Being is on the rack being stretched, again tortured. It is seen that this Being has had several other life cycles of religious persuasion, but the only scenes being shown are of strange religious practices. Those karmic lessons were not learned in this lifetime. He will obviously reincarnate, and there will be a life cycle in which he will be able to resolve his religious misunderstanding, but it may not be in the immediate next life. It may take more than one life.

Paul's father has passed on, but from everything I've been told about his father, the man had a great deal of anger and frustration, raping Paul's stepsister when she was quite young. With a past life pattern of self-flagellation, this would leave a residue of much anger in the cells. This was particularly interesting to me as a therapist, because when Athor did some past life readings for a Catholic priest who has a history in this lifetime of sexually abusing many children, his past life pattern showed many lifetimes of flagellation in religious settings. My theory is the stored-up anger results in energy which comes out in future lives as misused sexual energy.

Evelyn: Let's move on to Paul's next question. Paul was a minister for nineteen years. What was the purpose in his being a minister in this lifetime?

Athor: It is seen that in past cycles, religious persuasions paid a more important role than in some people's lives. There appears to be a Christian life in which he is in some kind of desert, and is dressed in rags basically. This could have been at the time of Christ. He is trying to get through the desert, but is quite thirsty and tired. There were other people too making this trek through this remote desert area. Some of them did not make it through the desert because there was no water, etc. Others survived because they finally were able to walk far enough, and found some water in an oasis.

Paul felt guilty in that life because it appears that he was the leader of this small group of people following him through the desert. Actually it wasn't so much that he felt guilty, but he felt responsible for those people, since they were part of his congregation in this lifetime. It appears there have been two or three other lifetimes, not necessarily involving a group of people. There was one where he was some type of monk in a monastery, and spent much time alone in studies and concentration. So he has had a few life cycles dealing with religious persuasions, all of them except for one were of a Christian type of belief.

Evelyn: Paul would like to know more about the lifetime between us, when he was a soldier and I was a young boy. (This may be some repetition, but that is necessary to get back into that lifetime. As usual, I state both names again.) I was a young boy, and he was a relative. He was with a band of soldiers. Paul was the leader of a group of soldiers; they took me hostage and strung me up on a tree somehow. He really didn't intend to kill me, and I finally got away.

Athor: This appears to be the cycle wherein they were after someone, and they split up and went off in different directions. A small group of men in the woods tried to encircle this other individual. He unknowingly had been involved, because another individual talked him into it. The boy was too young, and so he took sides unwittingly, not knowing what was really going on. The present Paul being was in that group of men who were trying to find the other one, and they came across you, the young boy. Basically, Paul in that life wanted to teach you a lesson because you had gone astray in a sense by taking sides and going with this other individual. He wanted to teach you a lesson. It seems as though those were the times and the manners in which people taught certain lessons.

There seems to be an over powering energy that Paul wanted the boy to understand; that he had picked the wrong side, so to speak. He had gone on the wrong track. This was a warning. This was a lesson to not go down that road, or pick that track-type of thing; not to be in league with the other individuals. It is seen that you went back to that village where you had come from, and went to your home further into the woods when you were let go. This would appear to be somewhere between the 17 and 18 hundreds, in the area of Italy.

Evelyn: What can you tell Paul about his sickness as a small child, and having to stay very close to the house and do so much of the housework while his brother got to work in the fields? (Athor then asked for the name of his mother.)

Athor: First of all, we feel a great, great sadness and emotional turmoil from this experience. We would like to say that all experiences that are encountered on this Planet Earth are learning experiences. They are the soul's attempt to gain further knowledge, but mostly wisdom. And part of wisdom is the understanding of one's life lessons. In that understanding there is a freeing and liberation when the lesson has been learned; this is equivalent to the being's understanding of the soul.

In the case of Paul's early life experience, it is seen that there were excessive tendencies in his nature carried over from other cycles as an independent spirit; not to say there is anything wrong with an independent spirit, but there were some excesses in past cycles of that independence. It started going a little too far off on one side, so that rather than gaining strength and learning the positive strengths on the side of independence, it was leaning in the direction of being too self-centered. Paul's soul wished to right that, balance that out, to not have that go too far on one end, so to speak, so that the independence of his spirit would not become self-centered and self-serving.

Because of Paul's religious life cycles there are a lot of factors here. The religious life cycles have played a great role in his soul's history of incarnating on this planetary system. They have shaped and helped make the choices of which cycles he would experience, and what type of circumstances he would encounter. Here again we see that it was the soul trying to balance any further excess. There is a lot involved. It is not just the decision to right itself and not go to the extreme. It did it in an abrupt, concentrated and dramatic fashion because of the life cycles of religious beliefs. If Paul had not had those religious incarnations, it would not have been so abrupt. There would have been many life cycles in which this potential of becoming too self-serving would have been balanced. It would not have been one seemingly fell swoop, such as in this lifetime. Basically, it is a lesson that this soul chose to prevent him from becoming too self-serving, but also because of life cycles with his mother from this lifetime. (Athor asks that both names be stated again.)

We have here a scene of where the woman is spanking a child. The child appears to be about three years old. She tells the child to go stand in the corner of a little hut where they live. There is a fire going to keep warm. The child is very defiant; even though he stands in the corner, the energy from the child is, "Well, I am going to get even." He finally goes outside to play. He goes into a wooded area that surrounds this little place. There are tall weeds, brush and trees further on, and there is a pond. He suddenly goes into the pond, and he is gasping because he is drowning, gasping for air and flaying about.

There is another child that appears, and comes and yanks him out of there, and this other child then brings him home to the mother. She is beside herself, very upset that he almost died, and she doesn't want to lose the child. However, she is also upset that he always seems in that life to do things that are harmful either to himself or to others in some way. So rather than showing her concern about his almost having drowned, she is angry, and lets the anger rule. She pulls him roughly back into the house and punishes him by demanding that he stand with his face to the wall again, and this time he has to stand there for a long time.

It is seen that still the energy in him is not one of remorse, because at that point he obviously felt that he had almost died, so why should he feel remorse. The mother is just frustrated, and can't bring out the emotions that she was concerned that he would have died, and to comfort him, and all that. The energy is just frustration, and so the energy sinks deeper into the child; that this is not fair, and these vengeful energies start forming and coming forth in the child. These vengeful energies were basically turned in on the child. It seems you have had a pattern in past cycles, partly because of the religious cycles, that when you became angry it turned in on yourself. It backfired on you inside in some fashion. So there are a lot of deep seeded scars, we hear, and deep seated hurt. All of your religious cycles camouflaged or buried these feelings.

We are seeing that in the religious cycles the main lesson that needs to resolve is the energy from those religious cycles in which there was almost a type of masochism. That is truly what the soul is seeking; it is the compassion and wisdom to blossom freely without these energies that are standing in the way and have created great turmoil and distress for Paul. So there is an element of self-forgiveness, with a capital S, which needs to come into play because of these past cycles wherein there were some basic misunderstandings connected with forgiveness, and with vengeance. Those two have been an issue for him as a being for several incarnations. As he begins to understand and see it in a truer light that a lesson is not synonymous with punishment.

In the usual traditional Christian teachings, unfortunately, the lesson and punishment are synonymous terms, but in truth that is incorrect. That is one of the things Paul had to come to understand and learn in this life cycle, by releasing this type of misunderstanding. There is much in the true Christian teachings which is very beneficial and enlightening, helpful and so forth. But there are also some aspects to Christian teachings which are not beneficial, and they lead one astray, and lead one into penance and feelings of guilt and/or holier than thou, or less than thou, and on and on and on. These are not true teachings. However, because they are so prevalent and wrapped up in what is considered Christianity, and has been for centuries, they have been accepted as the true teachings.

In Paul's cycles of primarily Christian lifetimes, he has been imbued with these teachings as truth. And so he has carried these beliefs for many lives. It is his soul's prerogative and job, basically, to balance this out. Whatever misunderstanding a being acquires in any given life cycle must be dissolved, must be released, because misunderstanding builds on misunderstanding, and then one gets so far away from the actual truth in the beginning that it is very difficult to wake up to what was the original truth in any given situation. And so this is what is being seen here regarding his experiences.

Evelyn: Paul has had bouts of severe depression in this lifetime. Can you tell us anything more about this?

Athor: There are many, many components to any given case. In this particular case we see some of the main components are of the religious cycles, and what was accepted in those cycles as being true, was not necessarily true. That is not to say that the beliefs were totally false, but by accepting certain elements in the religious cycles that were false he built a foundation of beliefs.

His beliefs were not built on a solid foundation. Because it was not solidly built, the foundation could not weather the storms; it would began to sway with the slightest tremor that hit his life, just as a building without a solid foundation will shake and often fall in an earthquake. Those belief systems needed to be dissolved and be replaced with a foundation of true beliefs in order to survive the storms of life.

Evelyn: Paul has what is called an essential tremor, mainly in his left hand. Can you give any insight on this physical problem?

Athor: Yes, it was an injury to the head; it appears to be in his youth or perhaps as a child. There is an area of the brain that has been affected. This is the part that is causing the tremor; a concussive type of injury left an imprint on the etheric body, which then came into the physical body. This relates to at least one past life cycle in which the being sustained a massive head trauma, and it was carried over into the present physical body. It appears that the being was struck by a solid object, almost like a beam. Somebody else was wielding this object, and he was struck in the head. The scene is on a sort of cliff-type scene, overlooking a beautiful body of water and valley, a beautiful area. The other individual struck him on the head and he rolled down the hill. He didn't appear to be dead in that life cycle, but there appears to be a lot of energy connected with that life.

It is seen that the use of a field biofeedback machine would help considerably, as this type of instrument works on etheric and other levels, wherein the energy can be more readily accessed and manipulated. When energy comes into the physical vehicle, and physical methods are utilized, that is essentially the slowest method. If the energies can be dissolved and removed from the etheric and other levels, even though it may not necessarily have an immediate physical effect, it will stop that chain reaction.

Evelyn: Is there anything else that you feel you need to add before we stop?

Athor: Yes. It is seen that Paul has had many life cycles wherein he strove to achieve a certain level, a certain goal. Because of this he has experienced much striving, struggling, and working toward an end to reach a goal. This is a positive aspect to his nature and to his energies. When times have been extremely rough, this energy has been his strength, but he has not utilized it enough in the sense of understanding its importance in his life. This is a very, very strong and positive quality in him, this goal-oriented and striving capacity which he has had in many life cycles.

So the message basically is to look more at the beauty of his nature and the strength that he possesses, rather than the weaknesses he may have felt and experienced; the traumas he may have experienced, and all these energies which seem to have plagued him for so long. They are not the true reality of who he is; he is not that person. Those are simply energies and qualities he has acquired through the incarnation process.

As Paul has come from lifetime to lifetime, he has picked up lint and dust from the road along the way. He is not the only one. This is the nature of life on Planet Earth. However, it is also the nature of the soul to be able to clean off that lint and dust, to let it go, and let the real being, the real inner being come forth and shine. He MUST understand that the lint and the dust are not him. All the traumas and the pain and the suffering are not him. He is much, much greater than that.

Evelyn: One more question. Is Paul one aspect of my soul?

Athor: An aspect indeed we can readily state.

Evelyn: Thank you very much. We will stop for now.

In attempting to understand all of this from my therapist point of view, I feel that Paul's sense of responsibility goes back many eons ago to the time when he was one of the leaders on an Off-Earth Council. As stated when discussing my soul relationship with Paul, he had to lay down some rules for the Council regarding some scientific work. Athor was not specific regarding the particular scientific work. Having conducted Athor readings for many clients, one may conclude that something drastic occurred, resulting in much loss of life, since this was a somewhat similar scenario for some of my clients who suffered from depression in this lifetime. These Councils dealt in powerful energies, and were never totally sure of the outcome of their experiments. The imprint from these disasters registered at a deep level upon the souls of those involved, resulting in continued feelings of guilt and responsibility for these disasters.

I have met other men who seemingly were also aspects of my soul. The initial attraction was always quite strong, but due to their choices for their particular past cycles, it soon became apparent that we were basically incompatible. Meeting one's twin soul (the other half of their soul when it is first created from the Source) is extremely rare, and I have never felt as if this were a possibility with any other human being I have known. Paul and I are so wonderfully compatible that I do think this is a possibility. If so, we are very fortunate to have met at this particular point in our lives, since I seriously doubt we would have been compatible at all earlier in this lifetime. I needed to really understand myself from a soul point of view, and Paul had to go through his Near Death Experience before we could feel these deep feelings for each other. There is obviously a larger purpose in our coming together, since I can assist Paul in understanding true spirituality thus once and for all, overcoming those false beliefs developed during his religious cycles. All of my metaphysical beliefs have been new to Paul, but he is totally open to learning and is eager to gain new knowledge.

I learned through my marriage to Wally that some people simply cannot accept new beliefs. The greatest difficulty in that marriage was my insistence that Wally at least try to understand my belief in reincarnation, but of course, with his particular past cycles this was an unrealistic expectation. I was careful to go slowly in exposing Paul to all of these "way out" cosmic understandings. It took him a very long time to read my book *From Sirius to Earth*, but I appreciated the fact that it is quite challenging reading for anyone who is new to metaphysics, and all along he would ask intelligent questions.

I then suggested he read *There is a River*, the story of the life of Edgar Cayce, the great American mystic. Next, he read a book about the life of Jesus, written by Jacelyn Eckman, who channels a being who was supposedly a close cousin of Jesus. I felt this would clarify some of the false teachings of the church that had been ingrained into Paul's consciousness during his past religious cycles. I have been delighted with Paul's eagerness to be a co-leader in the "Light" group we have formed here in Bandon. We hope that together we can assist in ushering in this new age of enlightenment for the Earth.

Chapter 21

Conclusions

Rainbow after storm

I feel that Paul is a very brave soul to allow me to write about his life and past life cycles. I believe that my first three husbands would also approve of my writing about their lives and our relationships, because I was extremely fortunate in being with men who always were proud of my work, even though they did not understand it.

I actually had no concept of metaphysics during my first marriage, but Carroll encouraged me to seek a Master's degree in Counseling, which was the first step toward all of my work in attempting to understand the human psyche. That was in 1963. Much later when I was on the Board of Directors of the Association of Past Life Regression Therapists (APRT - at the time, now known as IARRT – International Association for Regression Research and Therapies) required my being away from home a great deal during my marriage to Wally. In addition, I attended numerous conferences and presented many workshops. If Wally and I had enjoyed a close relationship I would no doubt have felt very guilty about being away from home so much, but as it was, it was one of the ways I coped with our very difficult last fourteen years of marriage. Looking back on that marriage, my experience with Wally was a huge step forward in my spiritual growth. When we are faced with adversity it motivates us to begin searching for a deeper meaning to life here on Earth.

Losing Ed after only ten years together was devastating, but after his death I realized that I was a much stronger person than I believed possible. I knew almost no one in Bandon, so I forced myself to do social activities which are rather against my nature, since I still feel I am basically a shy person, not making new friends easily. Also being the trustee of Ed's estate made me realize that I am a good business woman although that is not something I particularly enjoy doing.

Now that I have met Paul, neither of us wants to be apart. Paul and I each still have our own homes, and we alternate spending time at each place, although my cat, Boots, much prefers my place so he can roam freely in the yard. Whereas, at Paul's place which is on a bluff overlooking the river and ocean, we don't feel it is safe to let Boots out of the house. Consequently, we spend more time in my house rather than Paul's, even though he has fantastic views from his place.

When we occasionally spend a night alone, we always call each other around 9:00 PM, plus at any other time we feel so inclined. My point is that I cannot imagine ever spending much time away from Paul. We totally enjoy each other's company. I feel this is one of those rare relationships in which we have each been "gifted" by our souls. We hope this is because we have been evolving spiritually, and earned our wonderful mutual love. However, we both realize that we have only reached this point through all of the earlier relationships in our lives; therefore, we give thanks to all of the people who have made us who we are today. We are so grateful, and wish to assist other people in their own spiritual growth in any way we can.

So what does all of this mean in terms of your own soul growth and relationships?

The chief purpose of relationships is to assist each other in growing spiritually; to help each other evolve. This involves giving moral, loving support through all the trials and tribulations here on Planet Earth, often not an easy task. Older souls will often be attracted to younger souls because there is karma that needs to be balanced, and/or the younger soul needs the assistance from the older soul. Children will often be born to a couple who also have karmic issues with one or the other of the parents.

In my first husband Carroll's life he seemingly had karmic issues with his mother, who was always asking him for money. I believe their karma was balanced. Since he severely battered his two wives after his marriage to me, plus badly beating up one of his daughters to the point that his wife reported him to the police, I imagine that they will all need to meet at a future time to balance out their karma. Carroll reported the information about his later life to me when I saw him about a year before he passed over.

In Wally's situation, he had deep karmic issues with his younger daughter. He felt that she was the main reason for his divorce from his first wife. He also had karmic issues with his mother. I feel from what I observed that he balanced the soul issues with his mother, mainly because they both made many compromises. I doubt that the issues with his younger daughter were resolved, perhaps because they both were younger souls, and both determined that their way was the right way. I believe that Wally's mother was an older soul. It was difficult for her to be with Wally again as an only child, but she always seemed to support him, although there were obviously underlying conflicts.

In Ed's case, he had deep karmic issues with all of his three daughters. Although he tried to resolve issues, they were not willing to see anything from Ed's point of view. As stated in Athor's reading for Ed, all he could do was to bless them and send Light; he was not going to change them. In addition, he had many past life conflicts with his father. Again, there was no way that Ed was going to change his father. That negative relationship unfortunately continued up through the time his father passed over. He made many overtures toward his father during the time I was with him, but at "Pop's" funeral, it was evident that all of the old feelings toward his father came to the surface again. Ed's brother was mainly responsible for this, since his brother's eulogy at the service seemed to purposely paint a negative picture of Ed's relationship with his father. On the other hand, Ed's relationship with Lindy, his second wife, was a real gift. Despite her long bout with cancer, they apparently had a deep love for each other and very positive past life relationships, resulting in a relationship with no great strife.

His marriage to me entailed some conflicts, mainly because of a great difference in political persuasions; but past life experiences had been positive. Therefore, there was a basic respect and love for each other, despite very different personalities. I would like to think that Ed's relationship with me resulted in further spiritual growth for him, since I exposed him to many metaphysical concepts. He gave me a greater appreciation for men and women in the military, and gave me the courage to uproot my life in California to move to Oregon. Had I not made that move, I would never have met Paul, the only one of my husbands who makes me consistently happy and content.

When we first met, Paul told me a great deal about his past relationships from this lifetime. He still has difficulty believing that he actually chose his parents, particularly his father, about whom he has very little good to say. But since he left the family when Paul was quite young, he actually did not know his father very well, only having a fairly brief contact when he was already a young man. However, perhaps because of the poor example of his father, he has made strong overtures toward mending the relationship with his son and daughter, who were teenagers when he was divorced from his first wife. They have responded in kind; therefore, these relationships are being healed in this lifetime, with no further karmic obligations to meet in a future lifetime.

Paul was devastated by the negative turn of events in his second marriage, as well as a very bad relationship with his third wife. I am not even speculating on whether any of those souls will meet again; but as Paul and I have discussed, his entire life has helped him evolve into the kind, loving person he is today. Also, his long history of religious lives has probably prepared the way for him to genuinely see "The Light" about the true relationship of the soul to the Creator, the All That Is. He is totally ready to absorb as much knowledge as possible to help him in his further spiritual growth.

As for my own karmic family relationships, I chose a father with a very close soul relationship. We can have positive karma as well as negative karma with individuals. Unfortunately, I was only 29 when my father passed away. He was a bachelor until he was 40 years old, and I was not born until he was 42. I adored Boble (the name I gave him from the time I could talk and tried to pronounce his name of Noble.)

When I was 12, Boble wrote *A Constitution of the United Nations of the World*, published before the establishment of the United Nations. This no doubt had an influence on my later work. He only disciplined me twice in my life - once when my cousin and I were about 5 years old and had some matches in a large clothes closet, and the clothes caught on fire. The fire had to be put out with bucket brigades of water. The second time was when the same cousin and I disappeared for most of the day, and wandered off our 1000 acre farm property into the land of a neighbor who chased us off with a shotgun. We might have gotten away with it, but in order to run away quickly, I cut my leg crawling under a barbed wire fence. So we both decided to confess, since we were extremely frightened by the whole experience. Needless to say, we both learned our lessons well and felt that our punishment was justified. Boble and I had a past life as father and son, connected to the priesthood in South America. We shared a number of other past lives, but this was the only one in which I obtained definitive data.

While I knew my mother loved me, it was always understood in my family, at least by me, that my brother was her favorite child. My mother was often appalled by some of the things I did when I finally flew out of the nest, such as going to Japan, traveling with a man when we were not yet married (Wally,) wearing mascara, etc. etc. When I asked Dr. John about my relationship with her, he stated that she was my brother in my former life in England. I was then in a male incarnation. We were both tailors in a rather well-to-do family. My brother, aka my mother in this lifetime, was prone to get work done too fast, resulting in rather shoddy tailoring jobs. He/she was more interested in the material world than I. Something I did apparently upset my brother/mother and he/she died of a stroke. This obviously left some ill feelings toward me at a soul level. I understood our relationship from a soul level, always feeling from an early age that somehow I needed to protect my mother, never sharing any of my real feelings with her.

Mama was the ultimate "Southern Lady," very concerned about what other people thought in our small town. She was a member of the D.A.R. (Daughters of the American Revolution,) and quite active in the Presbyterian Church and the Garden Club. All of these were activities which did not appeal to me at all. However, I missed Mama a great deal after she died, and sincerely hope we have balanced out any karmic debt I may have owed her.

My relationship with my only sibling, a brother, has always been positive. What I have learned about our past lives made for a close relationship in this lifetime. He is a good traditional Christian, but accepts his way-out metaphysically-oriented sister without criticism. We don't have much in common, but we care a great deal about each other and keep in close contact.

Think about the people in your life. Your intuition can help you determine whether there is positive or negative karma between you, your family and friends. Then, think about the people you consider your enemies. They can often be our greatest teachers, since we learn more through tribulations than we do through lives that are calm, peaceful and lacking trauma. Sometimes my clients would go into a past life in which seemingly nothing very important happened. These are lives that give the soul time to rest before undertaking perhaps another series of lives filled with much tragedy and/or considerable challenges.

You no doubt have had many of these kinds of lives, but I question that anyone on our Planet at this present time in our evolution has a lifetime that is totally peaceful; in fact, many writers of metaphysics claim that we are being given major challenges one after another, either in our life circumstances or in relationship challenges. This is a sign that our evolution is now in warp speed. Just try to see all of these dramas as part of the long evolutionary process. One way or the other each person's evolution will continue beyond this existence here on this Planet. Many of my readers will no doubt have difficulty believing the Off-Earth existences I have cited for Wally, myself, Ed and Paul. They, in fact, still seem bizarre to me. I want to bring this down to a more believable example.

A friend sent his seventeen year old daughter to me for past life therapy with the hope that we could get some soul insight into her relationship with a young man who often abused her, although she was very much in love with him. After taking Julie's history, I did a numerology chart for her as I did for many of my clients. Interestingly, her destiny was 55, a master number, and one that is very rare. Numerologists actually know very little about the meaning of this number, but from what I have studied it appears to be indicative of a trance channel.

During the first hypnosis session it was very difficult to get Julie to talk, since she obviously was in a deep trance. She would only give me descriptive words when I asked her to describe the body she was in. She began with seeing a bright light, and later that was all she remembered of the regression. I finally realized that was all I was going to get from her were descriptive phrases, so I began asking her many detailed questions trying to discover what/who she thought she was. It appeared that she was describing a rock. As we continued, the rock seemed to disintegrate, and she became part of the ground. Now she was saying, "chest sucked in, empty, heavy below, lower body fat, feet tiny, ugly, can't fly, feathers, can't fly, too flat, heavy, soft, weird bird, no feet, half toes, ugly doesn't have wings." I asked her if she were some kind of extinct bird, and she replied, "Yes."

Our time was up, and I was frustrated because she still was not in a human body. She told me she didn't remember anything she said, so we didn't have much of a discussion about it, but made another appointment with the hope that she would finally become a human. I was blown away by this, having never had a client who had not evolved into a human yet. Actually, the fact she had great difficulty talking made sense, since in the existences described she had no vocal chords.

About three weeks later, Julie again quickly went into a deep trance state. Once again, she gave a description of being part of the ground. Then she began describing a squiggly, wobbly creature with no legs, soft, with little hair and no head. I surmised that it was some kind of aquatic fish. After that, she became an amphibious reptile that ate plants from the ground. There were other existences described that seem to be an evolutionary progression, but my notes are not clear enough to report on more of these descriptions.

It was not until our fourth session that Julie finally found herself in a body, but it seemed like the body of someone who perhaps lived on another planet. She said she had no clothes on; her legs were very skinny, and her arms were very long. She didn't need to eat anything, but lived off of air. Then, "My mind is able to travel. I am going up to the sky. I enjoy it. My head feels light and my body feels heavy." Then, she seemed to die and go up to the spirit world where it was very bright.

By then Julie was growing tired of the whole process, since she had no memory of these sessions, and I was obviously not able to receive any insight into her relationship with her boyfriend. I was fascinated by all of this from a research viewpoint, but I didn't want to waste any more of Julie's time. It is inconceivable to me that a 17 year old girl would make all of this up, particularly since she was in a deep hypnotic state. It would have been interesting for her to have had an Athor reading to look into the soul relationship between her and her boyfriend, but this was before I had met Athor. Julie was not interested in traditional talk therapy, and trying to reason with her was futile, since her father had certainly tried to talk her out of continuing this seemingly very negative relationship. I heard later that she had indeed married her boyfriend. He continued his abuse, and she finally fled out of state with her child to get away from him.

This experience certainly convinced me of the validity of the theory of evolution even before Athor started going into Off-Earth lives for my clients. So to me, there is no conflict between creationism and evolution. They are both plans of the Creator, the All That Is.

Our soul is created from a spark of God (Creator). This spark divides into many other sparks, each becoming part of our cosmic family (Religious Research term) also known as other aspects of our soul. Athor often described this event as looking much like a fireworks display through her psychic eyes. These sparks begin to go through various experiences in the universe. These first experiences are not determined by the souls at that point, but seem to be rather random.

The soul usually becomes an individualized entity when it incarnates on its home planet. Then the soul is able to make its own decisions about the path it will take during its evolutionary journey. I believe that we have a life plan, but have free choice, and don't always follow that life plan. Each person's path is somewhat different, depending on past lives, particular talents, and present spiritual development. We are all sparks of the Creator; let us honor that Divine Origin.

I want to end this with a recent message Paul wrote to me as he was looking out at the view below his home:

"My, how beautiful the colors are in every direction I look this morning. The ocean is a rich blue, as well as the river, as far as I can see toward the Hwy 101 Bridge. Greenery on the north side of the river is as rich as I have seen it. It seems as if Nature has decorated her creations in bright new clothing. Several fishing boats are out on the ocean; some just plodding around in a circle, probably over a nest of catchable fish; others are sailing along at a speed that suggests they are trolling for the 'big ones' of whatever species they might be. The temp is already above 60, and it looks like we may get a good bit more warmth today. I hope so!

Evelyn, life is good! Try to enjoy every day you have here on this beautiful Earth!"

Cherish the Earth, because you may have been part of the Earth (ground, as with Julie.) You may have been a worm, reptile, or maybe some weird creature Off-Earth in your own evolutionary path. We evolve, we progress, we learn, and we go on and on!!

We All are One!

Namaste

Epilogue

I have felt the need to publish this book by 2012, because I believe it contains material that can assist humanity in its evolvement. I sincerely believe that we are in a period of great transition. Although I greatly appreciate the many books published through Religious Research, I do not agree with the latest book, *The Plan of Love and Light,* by Helen Roberts. Helen, whom I know personally and greatly admire, writes about the second coming of Jesus. I believe that our transition to a higher vibration will be on an individual basis through raising the consciousness of each person. If enough people raise their consciousness we will have an effect on the entire Planet, as in the "12th monkey theory."

Having various Masters incarnate in past cycles has only worked to a certain extent to raise our consciousness. Invariably their original teachings have been distorted in certain individuals and groups quest for power. Dr. Loehr, the founder of Religious Research, was a minister and believed very strongly in a second coming of Christ, and Helen is reflecting his belief. This does not negate the other books of Religious Research nor the readings conducted by Dr. Loehr.

It is my personal belief that we will individually be expressing the Christ Consciousness mentality, sufficiently to see us through the present traumas manifesting now on the Earth with the least amount of turmoil possible. It is high time for changes. I am including some Athor material that I have had on my website for several years. It is even truer today than it was twelve years ago.

There are events occurring of monumental proportions. It is seen that the surface of your planetary sphere will greatly alter within a span of approximately fifteen to twenty-five years. There are many factors which are contributing to this; one being the ecosystem and the imbalances within it; another being the influx of so-called alien life forms. Within a period of approximately 15 years there will be massive and direct communication with so-called ETs that will no longer be hidden nor twisted in the media. This is not to say that the attempt will not be there, but the swell of consciousness will be such that in that time period it will be common knowledge that these life forms do indeed exist, and that they are here and have been for quite some time.

Each Being is now undergoing massive transformation, and those who cannot withstand the transforming energy currents will withdraw. Many are leaving the Planet, and that is just one aspect of that type of withdrawal. There is both an involutional and evolutional phase of cosmic energies coming through the atmosphere at this time. It is up to each individual to choose which one they wish to go with, so to speak, and the pressure is equal on both ends. This is one of the resultant phases of many cosmic occurrences and planetary shift changes, etc. in the greater scheme of things this has all been predicted and planned; not planned in a personal sense, but it has been in the ethers for quite some time for the evolution of this planetary system.

As these energies impinge upon the Earth sphere, each individual life unit upon the surface of this sphere is being radically affected. We are simply suggesting that you take a conscious stand as to how you are being affected by these energies, because it is a two-edged sword, and it is calling for awareness for those who wish to evolve. They must have the conscious desire to continue in their evolution, in their awareness. If this is given up, the involutionary energies, being equally strong, will predominate and bring about a contractive phase in all those Beings who do not take a stand within.

The cosmic energies will continually hit them and they will feel as if they are totally spaced out. They have no bearings, and they don't know which end is up. These, of course, are usually the more sensitive individuals who have already developed certain openings. The average mass humanity is experiencing this primarily in their economic strata and their daily struggles to remain alive. They are experiencing the results in their relationship issues, as well as in their economic levels of existence. Health issues are also being greatly brought to the surface.

These energies coming forth now are very, very potent cosmic energies, and they are designed to cleanse and purify; but in the process of cleansing and purifying, many Beings are feeling cut off from their Source. That is mainly due to the fact that it now requires a daily, conscious commitment, and daily conscious time spent in determining what the Beings' purpose in their life is. If they cannot come up with certain pictures, then it is recommended that they simply reaffirm their alignment with Light on a daily level. They must ask that the Christ energy and the God Force come through in whatever way is most meaningful and most productive. This is so the God

Force and the God Light can come through as fully as possible through those particular Beings.

We are now entering a level of creation wherein human beings are being asked to co-create. Those who do not choose to co-create in and with Light will not only suffer greatly, but will also feel as though they don't know anything anymore. That is indeed part of the cleansing, but is also an impetus to become aware, to co-create, to take a stand within, and align one's consciousness with that energy of Light. The ones who choose not to, and simply wish to continue their old patterns, will find that much is ripped away from their lives. It is not a gentle action. These energies are not namby pamby. They are very potent energies and rays. They are neither negative nor evil. They simply are very powerful in moving toward the Source.

Each Being, by realigning with that Source, is setting up a magnetic pole within them which will then allow many other energies to come and feed into that pole. By feeding into that pole, which is essentially through the spinal column; the Light bodies of each one of those beings so consciously choosing to align with the Light will become very, very powerful and energized. This is the transitional phase which is occurring for those who so choose it; to transform, one could almost say from one species to the next. This is happening on very deep inner levels; but those who are very sensitive are feeling this on all levels.

It simply requires a conscious thought of that commitment to Light. Seek to communicate with the Light and you will not be disappointed. It might not come in the manner in which you expect, but you will always get an answer, whether it is through feelings, thoughts, etc. We cannot stress strongly enough a daily commitment to the Light. To be utilized by the Christ Force as a vehicle of Light in helping others is now of paramount importance.

Athor – December 5, 1999

We are at a time of great changes on Planet Earth. We need to ASK for assistance from the Beings of Light. They will not interfere unless asked to help just as you should ask for help from your guides and guardian angel. Please use the following visualization daily with a partner or group.

Visualize a ring of fire or white Light with rainbow colors swirling around us (or a group). Place the planet Earth in the center of this circle. We ask for all the beings of Light who wish to assist in bringing peace, harmony, good will, unity and balance to this planet to do so. We invoke the highest levels of Light to protect Earth and all of its inhabitants.

Channeled from Athor, via Aki, December 2010

This is quite simple and can be memorized very easily. My soul mate, Paul and I do this daily, usually right before a meal prior to asking the blessing. We would deeply appreciate the readers of this book joining us in spreading this message to other inhabitants of the Earth.

I want to leave my readers with a beautiful passage which is a quotation at the beginning of *From Sirius to Earth:*

"Many Beings do not realize what a grand and glorious place this Planet Earth can be. They do not realize that it is not simply a school for those who have not yet learned, but rather a most marvelous testing ground for the souls and Beings of every level and plane unto the Godhead itself.

Do not look upon yourselves as limited creatures, as limited Beings, for you are all the same. You are all dancing lights in the infinite firmament of God. Each of you twinkles and radiates as the stars in the heaven do.

Those of you who suffer here, and wish perhaps that you were elsewhere, look out upon the night sky. Look out upon the twinkling stars up in the Father's heaven and know that is indeed what you all are; you are there as well as here. And indeed you are everywhere."

Athor, channeling the Christ Consciousness

About the Author

Evelyn Fuqua holds a B.A. in Psychology from Agnes Scott College, an M.A. in counseling from California State University Sacramento and a Ph.D. in Psychology from the Professional School of Psychology. She was a teacher, resource specialist and counselor in the public schools. Dr. Fuqua has presented many workshops at professional conferences. She served on the Board of Directors of the Association of Past life Research and Therapy (presently International Association for Regression Research and Therapies) and as State Relations Chairman for the California State Counselors Association.

Fuqua is the author of *From Sirius to Earth: A Therapist Discovers a Soul Exchange* and *You are Wonderful*, a manual on self-esteem for children.

Formerly in private practice in Rocklin, California, Dr. Fuqua is currently enjoying retirement on the Oregon coast with her mate Paul and their cat Boots.

31237919R00152

Made in the USA
Lexington, KY
03 April 2014